bonn's eastern policy
1964–1971

Bonn's Eastern Policy 1964-1971

Evolution and Limitations

by LASZLO GÖRGEY

International Relations Series Number Three
Published on behalf of the Institute of International Studies
University of South Carolina

ARCHON BOOKS · 1972

Library of Congress Cataloging in Publication Data

Görgey, Laszlo, 1921-
 Bonn's eastern policy, 1964-1971.

 (International relations series, no. 3)
 "Published on behalf of the Institute of International Studies,
University of South Carolina."
 Bibliography: p.
 1. Germany (Federal Republic, 1949-   )–Foreign relations–
Europe, Eastern. 2. Europe, Eastern–Foreign relations–Germany
(Federal Republic, 1949-   ). 3. Brandt, Willy, 1913-   I. Title.
II. Series: International relations series (Columbia, S. C.) no. 3.
DD259.4.G573   327.43'047   70-39727
 ISBN 0-208-01272-9

contents

foreword

On December 10, 1971, German Chancellor Willy Brandt was awarded the coveted Nobel Peace Prize in Oslo. Forty-five years before, in 1926, the only other German statesman so honored, Gustav Stresemann, had received the award for his work in the Locarno settlements. Like his predecessor Brandt had been German Foreign Minister (1966–1969), but he had gone on to the position of head of the Federal Republic. Both men sought to bury hatreds of the past and to find a way to overcome contemporary distrusts.

Brandt's *Ostpolitik*, a continuation of the work begun by Konrad Adenauer, has kindled high hopes in the Eastern European capitals as well as in the increasingly consolidated Western part of the continent. Yet, there is reason in times of such optimism to recall history and raise cautions. At the time of the "spirit of Locarno" for which Stresemann received his Nobel Peace Prize there was the same thrust for disarmament talks and plans which in some respects paralleled the SALT negotiations forty-five years later. The gentle but hard-minded Yale historian Hajo Holborn has noted, "In reality Locarno did not create a secure foundation of a European peace. It covered up certain deep cracks that had appeared in the building, but failed to repair the structural weaknesses. . . . It was a tragic failure to believe that eastern Europe could be neglected politically and economically without courting the gravest dangers. Even worse was the unfounded belief that international conflicts would dissolve if the states scuttled their armaments."[1]

Even Chancellor Brandt himself, while trying to pay that necessary attention to building the economic and social ties to eastern Europe, has been aware that Bonn's Eastern Policy of which he is now the major engineer on the scene is fraught with difficulties. At a speech in Stockholm two days after his honor in Oslo he recognized that organizing peace in Europe "is hard work on stony ground." He had been Mayor of Berlin on that fateful day in 1961 when the Berlin Wall was erected, and the Wall still stands. It may be a trifle more porous as a result of the Four Power Agreement of September 3, 1971 and the subsequent negotiations between the two Germanies, but it, like the hardened and militarily patrolled border through Germany symbolizes a continuing chasm in political systems East and West.

It is the fundamental political confrontation to which Dr. Laszlo Görgey calls our attention in his analysis of Bonn's policies toward the Communist East of Europe. His work, based on long and practical, not to mention bitter, experience under the political systems of both Hitler and Stalin, can serve as a healthy antidote for some of the seemingly unrealistic euphoria during what President Nixon has called a new "Age of Negotiation." Dr. Görgey wisely warns, "the acceptance of the status quo does not miraculously eliminate tensions — it may only temporarily defuse them. Nor does present Soviet diplomacy indicate that the alleged Soviet readiness for a European security arrangement represents more than a *tactical* change in the otherwise inflexible strategy of Soviet foreign policy." [p. 170]

Willy Brandt would agree with Professor Görgey's conclusion that to "ensure success in future dealings with the Soviet Union, East Germany and Eastern Europe, Bonn will not only need to have its conciliatory attitudes reciprocated from the East, but will also need continuous and strong political and moral support from the West." [p. 172] The German Chan-

1. Hajo Holborn, *The Political Collapse of Europe* (New York: Knopf, 1954), pp. 133–34.

cellor told the Bundestag on October 28, 1969, "The North Atlantic alliance, which has proved its worth now over a period of twenty years, will in future, too, provide a guarantee for our security. The unbroken unity of the alliance is a precondition for joint efforts to arrive at a *détente* in Europe." The central problem for Bonn as well as for Washington and other Western capitals is whether their unity can carry through and still lend encouragement to those measures related to attempts to reduce tensions and build the prospects for peace.

It should not be necessary after Hungary in 1956 or Cuba in 1962 or Czechoslovakia in 1968 to raise cautions about the nature of the Soviet system and unchanging Soviet goals and perspectives. Yet there are many today who would just as soon treat hopes as realities and for them Dr. Görgey's analysis of Bonn's Eastern Policy provides essential background information and insight.

Laszlo Görgey is a Research Associate of the Institute of International Studies at the University of South Carolina, and this volume is the third in a series of major studies sponsored by the Institute; the first, *Aspects of Modern Communism*, edited by Richard F. Staar was published in December, 1968; the second, *Prospects in the Pacific*, edited by the undersigned, will appear in April 1972.

RICHARD L. WALKER
James F. Byrnes Professor of
International Relations
University of South Carolina

February 1972

introduction

In many respects the Federal Republic of Germany occupies an enviable position in the family of nations. It ranks high among the industrialized countries, is the third greatest trading nation in the world, and it has the most stable economy in Western Europe. The new Germany contributes the largest single contingent of conventional forces to the North Atlantic Treaty Organization. Domestic stability has made it a reliable ally. Its phenomenal recovery from the physical and spiritual devastations of the Second World War stands unparalleled in post-war Europe. Yet this viable state, established during the classical period of the Cold War and in the shadow of the Iron Curtain, represents only a part of the German nation. Germany's division, along with that of Europe, has been the main stumbling block that has rendered an East-West understanding impossible.

West Germany's foreign policy has, by contrast, been circumscribed by unique conditions that could hardly be called enviable. Both the Soviet Union's intransigence and Konrad Adenauer's preference long dictated a foreign policy based exclusively on ties with Western Europe and the United States through strong NATO and Common Market organizations. By the mid-sixties, however, the assumptions upon which this policy was predicated clearly had to be re-examined. Not only had NATO become structurally weaker and politically less cohesive, it was also increasingly clear that West Germany's allies would not grant her the right to participate in strategic planning and to possess nuclear armaments jointly with other NATO partners. De Gaulle's policies at once frustrated Bonn's hopes for full partnership in a politically and economically integrated Western Europe, and made Bonn's position *vis-à-vis* the United States anomalous. As the Adenauer era drew to a close, the need for major foreign policy alternatives was apparent, for Bonn was faced with the distinctly alarming prospect of increasing isolation.

Certain developments made it appear possible at that time that Bonn might indeed be able to forge a new foreign policy, more appropriate to the changing international situation. During the early and mid-1960's the atmosphere of the Cold War in Europe had subsided and there were signs of the gradual erosion of the political unity in East Europe as well as in the West. Politically important men in both camps frequently expressed the desire for a re-evaluation of the European political relations, with an eye at least to evolving policies of far greater mutual accommodation, however distant from full reconciliation these might be.

Although the Soviet Union did not join in these tentative proposals, there were signs that the Kremlin's hold on Eastern Europe had become less firm. The foreign policies of some of the Communist states were characterized by increasing flexibility, if not of genuine independence. The Eastern Europeans' new freedom to maneuver was limited both by the interest of the Soviet Union and by those of the East European political elites themselves, to be sure. And yet the new situation gave West Germany an opportunity to try to follow a more imaginative foreign policy in East Europe, to offset their disappointments in the West.

The area within which the West in general, and the Federal Republic in particular, could maneuver was similarly circumscribed. Soviet hegemony over Eastern Europe and congenital distrust of German intentions in Poland and Czechoslovakia were major obstacles to the development of new initiatives. Germany's almost complete integration into the Western camp and the intransigent policies it had followed under the Hallstein

Doctrine further inhibited moves toward the normalization of relations. Last but not least, Germany's uneasy friendship with de Gaulle and the latter's penchant for power politics reminiscent of the late 19th century made the already delicate situation even more precarious for the West Germans.

In 1966, after much procrastination and much political stocktaking, the West German government initiated its new foreign policy toward Eastern Europe. The primary objective was to create a "spirit of Locarno," a lasting spirit of reconciliation which could lead to normal diplomatic and political relations between West Germany and her Eastern neighbors. The opening toward the East was an entirely new approach, for, in contrast to previous policies, it included as many concessions as were deemed possible under the circumstances. The new policy was not confined to Eastern Europe; it aimed equally at exploring the possibility of more normal relations between the two Germanies. Perhaps the most dramatic evidence of West Germany's new stance was its willingness to relegate the vexed question of reunification to second place and to give primary consideration to negotiations on other matters. The Kiesinger-Brandt coalition's new Eastern policy may be described without exaggeration as the most imaginative and realistic formulated by any West German government since the establishment of the Federal Republic.

After some initial success circumstances beyond West Germany's control brought the new policy to a standstill. The armed intervention of the Warsaw Pact in Czechoslovakia and its *ex post facto* justification in the Brezhnev Doctrine created a deadlock which lasted a full year. Prospects for further progress did not brighten until 1969, when after more than fifty years spent in opposition, the Social Democratic Party aided by the FPD (Free Democratic Party of Germany) came to power unencumbered by its previous alliance with the Christian Democrats and Christian Socialists.

With the establishment of the new government Bonn's approach to East Europe and the Soviet Union entered a new and probably decisive phase. Chancellor Brandt's new Eastern policy does of course resemble that followed by the Kiesinger-Brandt coalition — one could even say that it is a logical extension of that line. However, while overall objectives have remained unchanged, the assumptions underlying the new approach are so different and the changes in priorities so great that one could indeed talk about an entirely new policy. The Federal Republic under Willy Brandt is willing to make far-reaching and specific concessions to the Kremlin in lieu of an ambiguous "normalization" of its relations with Moscow, Pankow, and eventually with Eastern Europe. The new government's seriousness of intent is evident in its repeated efforts to reopen direct communications with Moscow, its acceptance of Moscow's "two Germanies" doctrine, and its apparent acquiescence in present European boundaries.

Few would deny that, united or divided, Germany is a vital force in the world today — and that the policies of the West German government are a major and increasingly important factor in determining the nature of international politics in the North Atlantic area in particular. The foreign policy of West Germany is a subject worthy of the most careful scrutiny.

The purpose of the present study is twofold. First an attempt will be made to shed some light on those foreign and domestic forces which were decisive in the evolution of Bonn's new Eastern policy. Moscow alleged that this policy was designed to undermine Soviet predominance in East Europe. The study's second purpose is to take a hard look at this response and that of the other East European states. Special attention will be given to East Germany.

The book is correspondingly divided into two parts. Chapters one through four describe the gradual development of West Germany's radical new Eastern policy, from the cautious beginnings under Erhard to maturation and implementation. The second part, chapters five through seven, analyzes the reactions of the various East European states and of the Soviet Union to the unprecedented overtures from Bonn.

The study is the result of research conducted partly in West Germany and partly in Eastern Europe. The generosity of the Relm Foundation and of the Institute of International Studies of the University of South Carolina enabled me to spend considerable time in 1966, 1968, and 1970 at the Free University of Berlin, at the Institut für Demoskopie at Allensbach and at the Academy of Sciences in Budapest. My research in West Germany included interviews and informal conversations with leading personalities of the two major political parties. I gathered invaluable information from interviews with prominent representatives of international trade and industrial development in Hungary. Active participation in international conferences jointly sponsored by the Foundation for Foreign Affairs and by Studiengesellschaft für mittel- und osteuropäische Partnerschaft also helped to broaden my political horizons and proved an excellent source of information.

No author can properly thank everyone for their assistance while writing his first book. I owe too much to too many in the preparation of the present study. First and foremost, I should like to acknowledge my deep indebtedness to Richard L. Walker, my friend, mentor and Chairman of the Department of International Studies at the University of South Carolina for his never ceasing encouragement and moral support when most needed. With regard to the manuscript his suggestions, of both a substantive and editorial nature, were invaluable.

I am also more than grateful to the Relm Foundation, to the Southern Council on International and Public Affairs, and to the Institute of International Studies at the University of South Carolina for their generous financial support of my research trips to Europe without which this study could not have been written.

A very special moral indebtedness must be registered to the Hon. Dudley Crawford Sharp, former Secretary of the Air Force and to his wife who after the Hungarian Revolution in 1956 opened up their hearts and home to two Hungarian refugees and started them on their difficult road toward a free and better life in the United States.

I also should like to extend my thanks to my colleagues, especially to Professor Paul W. Blackstock at the University of South Carolina and to Mrs. Susanne McCarthy of Yale University, whose critical comments and stylistical suggestions greatly enhanced the value of this work. Heartfelt appreciation goes to Mrs. Cloris De Groot, secretary at the Department of International Studies of the University of South Carolina, for her unselfish help in typing several drafts of the manuscript and in preparing it for publication.

Last but not least, tolerance and consideration in a family are a scholar's indispensable assets. I cannot express how much I owe my wife. Without her encouragement, tolerance and consideration I could not have begun this project, nor could I have carried it through.

LASZLO GÖRGEY

bonn's eastern policy
1964–1971

the
emerging pattern

The Quest for a "modus vivendi"

Germany occupies a strategic central position in Europe. This fact of geography, both a curse and a blessing, has inevitably had a major impact on the political thinking of the German nation. Any state in such a position has opportunities for trade or conquest in every direction, but it is also endangered on all sides unless it is able to main friendly relations with its neighbors.

Germany's geographic position has frequently made a policy of "no permanent commitments" either to East or West seem attractive to her leaders. Bismarck tried to preserve the balance between East and West in the interests of national security. In different degrees, this sort of reasoning also colored German policy both under the Weimar Republic and under Hitler. After the Second World War there were strong sentiments in favor of a new version of the same international posture, which were decisively overruled only when Chancellor Adenauer himself committed Germany firmly and publicly to the West.

From the early 1960's, one could sense rising dissatisfaction with the one-sided orientation of German foreign policy toward the West and an inclination to establish some sort of counterbalance in the East. However, neither an Eastern policy on the Bismarckian pattern nor even in the tradition of the Weimar Republic is possible for today's Germany. These two historical variations of German Eastern policy are not feasible for a number of reasons. A radical reorientation is difficult first because the Federal Republic had made a definitive choice between East and West for over twenty years. Moreover, this choice — although endorsed by the overwhelming majority of the population — was dictated by circumstances beyond the control of the Germans themselves. Prominent among these, of course, was Soviet hostility. Moscow had hoped to use the Soviet Occupation Zone as a base for political expansion throughout Germany, and was in any case a priori opposed to any German state not under Communist influence. The increasingly uncompromising attitude of the Soviet Union and its satellites eventually forced the Federal Republic to side with the Western powers. In the immediate postwar years Germany had no alternative to seeking security through integration with the West.

When West German planners laid the foundations of a postwar foreign policy in the aftermath of defeat and within the control of the Cold War, their goals of necessity were not very ambitious.[1] German planners aimed, first, to re-establish the state's sovereignty and freedom of action in international affairs; second, to secure the state against possible invasion from the East, and against *coup d'état* conducted subversively from within; and third, to contribute to the strengthening of Europe through close economic and political cooperation.

European integration was intended to create a common front for defense against Soviet aggression through the merger of military and economic potentials within free Europe. Strength and unity, it was hoped, would further provide the Western powers and Bonn with a favorable starting point for negotiations concerning the future of Germany. Inherent in this general program was the complex problem of priorities. Which should come first, integration or reunification? Adenauer chose "reunification through detour:" while seeming to press for re-

1. Wilhelm G. Grewe, *Deutsche Aussenpolitik der Nachkriegszeit* (Deutsche Verlagsanstalt, Stuttgart, 1960), p. 91.

unification, he bent every effort to quickening the pace of European integration by committing Germany militarily and economically to that end.

Adenauer's policy — called a policy of "no alternatives" by the postwar leader of the Social Democratic Party — has neither helped move toward reunification of the country, nor toward better accommodation with Germany's Eastern neighbors. There is no doubt that under Chancellor Adenauer West Germany had played an indispensable role in European security and that Bonn's domestic political stamina must be attributed in large measure to the successes of his foreign policy. But the cost of an exclusively Western-oriented policy was *immobilisme* toward the Soviet bloc, more particularly toward the East European countries. The nature of Bonn's commitments to the West virtually precluded an active Eastern policy. Yet responsibility cannot be placed entirely on the former Chancellor, whose political realism is conceded even by his enemies. Any criticism of Adenauer's foreign policy record in the 1950's must consider what alternative policies might have been more successful.[2]

The inflexibility of Germany's Eastern policy in this period is attributable not only to Chancellor Adenauer, but to the Soviet Union as well. While it is true that the USSR proposed a plan for the reunification of Germany in 1952 its conditions were patently unacceptable to both West Germany and her Western Allies.[3] Moreover, by forcing the military, ideological and economic integration of the East European states into the Soviet system, by denying the West economic access to this

2. An excellent evaluation of Germany's international position in the 1950's may be found in H. G. von Studnitz, "Deutschland Zwischen den Mächten," *Aussenpolitik*, August, 1956, pp. 481 ff.
3. *Europa Archiv*, May 1952, SD 10115–22, *Wortlaut der Sowjetnote an den Vereinigten Staaten, Frankreich, England und die Bundesrepublik am 10. März, 1952* (Bonn, 1952). In contrast to the 1952 proposal the Kremlin in 1959 came forward with a plan which on the one hand called for a peace treaty with a *divided* Germany, and on the other hand encouraged Ulbricht to suggest a confederation of the "two German states." To this see: *Europa Archiv*, November 10, 1959, SD 13251–64, *Wortlaut der Sowjetnote an die Bundesrepublik und des Friedensvertragsentwurfes vom 12. März, 1959* (Bonn, 1959). Cf. for an excellent analysis of this issue Boris Meissner, "Soviet Concepts of Peace and Security" in David S. Collier and Kurt Glaser (eds.), *The Conditions for Peace in Europe* (Public Affairs Press, Washington, D.C., 1969).

area, and waging an ongoing propaganda campaign against the Federal Republic, the USSR created an atmosphere which made serious bargaining impossible. The legacy of the Adenauer era has not been an easy one to overcome. The "policy of strength," the "policy of detour," and the Hallstein Doctrine,[4] and West Germany's uneasy marriage with France were all part and parcel of the politics of the Cold War. Yet the Adenauer era gave West Germany a feeling of being both needed and respected within the Western system. Finally, by successfully keeping alive the hope of the majority of the Germans that a satisfactory solution would be found to the national problem Adenauer provided domestic optimism conclusive to reinforcing West Germany's fragile democracy in the 1950's.

By the end of the Adenauer era German foreign policymakers came to feel that the Adenauer-Dulles policy toward the Soviet Union and Eastern Europe had outlived its usefulness. The "policy of strength" had not brought West Germany one iota closer to the ultimate aim of every German statesmen since World War II — the reunification of the divided country. In the mid-1960's the need for a significantly altered foreign policy posture was more and more widely recognized. These feelings were amplified by the growing opinion in many quarters that Bonn was in something of a political "cul de sac" vis-à-vis the West. De Gaulle added to the uneasiness of the West Germans by assuming that the Franco-German Friendship Treaty of January, 1963, could be used to further French foreign policy objectives toward the Western Alliance. President Kennedy's rapprochement with Moscow tended to bypass West German priorities and similarly suggested the premises upon which the Federal Republic's foreign policies were built might not apply. In sum, Bonn faced the prospect of political isola-

---

4. Under the Hallstein Doctrine the Federal Republic has warned that it will break off diplomatic relations with any nation that recognizes the East German regime. For a detailed discussion of the Hallstein Doctrine, see: Grewe, op. cit., pp. 138 ff, and Werner Zoll, "Ueber den Wert des Hallstein Doktrins," Aussenpolitik, September, 1966, pp. 602–10. The ineffectiveness of the Doctrine has been discussed by Wolfgang Wagner, "Überprüfung des deutschen politischen Instrumentariums: Die Hallstein Doktrin nach Ulbrichts Besuch in Aegypten," Europa Archiv, March 1965, pp. 157–66.

tion. Most depressing for the Germans perhaps was the fact that the Western Powers, contractually responsible for Germany's reunification, had failed to approach the Soviet Union with any concrete proposals since 1959.[5]

West German leadership must have been particularly distressed by the demonstrable reluctance of the Western powers, particularly the United States, to coordinate their policies toward Moscow and Eastern Europe with Germany. Pressured by Moscow's greater emphasis on its "two states" doctrine and by East Germany's partially successful diplomatic offensive in the non-aligned world, in February and April, 1964, the West German government itself pressed the Western powers to show renewed vigor in their German policy. Bonn hoped to confront the Kremlin with a clear-cut Western position concerning the futility of the Soviet "two-Germanies" theory.[6]

These West German overtures were not well received. Washington, London, and Paris all felt the time was particularly inopportune for reopening the German question. Bonn's allies argued that the deepening Sino-Soviet rift made the Soviet Union more anxious than ever to keep secure in Eastern Europe. But perhaps their overriding consideration was the probability that raising the German question would in and of itself be considered a provocative move by the Soviets — at a time when the word *détente* had a certain hopeful magic about it in western capitals.

As Bonn began to review its policy options in earnest, it must have been a foregone conclusion that for economic considerations and for the sake of national security West Germany would remain basically Western-oriented. Within this framework, however, the country's unsettled relations with Eastern Europe became a primary concern. The establishment of a modus

---

5. The last of these concrete proposals was the Herter Plan. It proposed a step-by-step approach toward German reunification coupled with proposals for European disarmament and security. The Plan was rejected *in toto* by the Soviet Union. For a full text of the Herter Plan, see *Department of State Bulletin*, Vol. XL, No. 1040, June 1, 1959, pp. 775–81.

6. The German move was considered as ill-timed and meaningless, even in German political circles. The *Neue Zürcher Zeitung*, May 2, 1964, p. 1, quotes Herbert Wehner saying that "under the present situation in the Communist Camp, there is not the slightest chance for a factual and earnest discussion of the German question."

vivendi with her Eastern neighbors had been and might be difficult in the future, but by the mid-1960's at least partial normalization on this front had become a virtual political imperative. De Gaulle's flirtation with the Kremlin, France's increasing contacts with Eastern Europe, and President Johnson's announcement of building "bridges of trade, of visitors and of humanitarian aid"[7] across the gulf separating Eastern Europe from the West only made the rethinking of their own policy more vividly urgent to West German leaders.

Immediate establishment of formal diplomatic relations with Eastern European states in 1964 was politically unfeasible for a variety of reasons, however. On one hand, neither the CDU/CSU and FDP coalition-government, nor its Social Democratic opposition, was willing to pay the price for prompt reconciliation. Poland and Czechoslovakia would not even have consented to exploratory discussions with Bonn before the acceptance of the Oder-Neisse Line as the final boundary between Poland and Germany and the repudiation of the 1938 Munich Agreement. Most importantly of all, West Germany was in no sense prepared to renounce the Hallstein Doctrine, a move which would have enhanced the international position of the rival East German government in that it would have been tantamount to stating that Bonn no longer claimed to be the sole representative of the German nation. The West Germans avoided an impasse by proceeding with a cautious policy which would pave the road toward gradual reconciliation. Among the most important features of the new policy was re-establishment and extension of trade relations with some of the Eastern European states.

Intensified Trade with the East

Prior to the war, East Europe and the Balkan states had been the most important trading partners of the German Reich. In the late 1950's, when the impact of polycentrism began to be felt, it was only natural that the Germans should attempt to in-

7. For the full text of President Johnson's speech at Lexington, Virginia, see *Department of State Bulletin*, Vol. L, No. 1303, June 15, 1964, *Dedication of George C. Marshall Library; Remarks of President Johnson.*

crease trade in these areas. Although both sides were willing to increase the volume of trade Germany nevertheless labored under some important handicaps.

In the 1930's, Nazi Germany was the largest single market for products from southeastern Europe and used its monopoly power of a single buyer to extract favorable terms of trade from sellers. Because of Germany's advantageous position and the diminishing absorptive capacity of other Western markets, the export industries of the Balkan countries suffered.[8] During the 1930's and World War II Germany used another kind of economic lever which left deep scars on both the economies and the national consciousness of these countries. Under the leadership of Dr. Hjalmar Schacht, Nazi Germany took advantage of the bilateral clearing system which was a result of elaborate exchange controls invoked during the Great Depression to dictate prices to its trading partners. While the East European states of the 1930's were better off with the type of trade the Third Reich imposed upon them than without any trade at all,[9] these highhanded economic policies left a legacy of suspicion and hatred toward Germany in the Balkans.

In spite of the fact that Adenauer's government had taken no official economic initiatives toward Germany's Eastern neighbors and in spite of bitter memories of past economic exploitation, trade with the Soviet Union's former satellites shows a steady increase from the late 1950's on. The direction and fluctuation of trade between West Germany and the four countries selected for statistical evaluation — Czechoslovakia, Poland, Hungary, and Rumania — are shown below in Table I.

Except for small declines in the value of exports to West Germany in 1959 and 1963, trade between these Communist states and West Germany has grown steadily. Of particular interest is the remarkable increase in volume of trade between West Germany and Rumania: at the end of 1961 annual trade in both directions was valued at $110.1 million, as against $41.4 million in 1959. Increases in West German trade with these three Communist states continued in both directions in

8. See Charles P. Kindleberger, *International Economics* (R. D. Irwin, Homewood, Ill., 1958), pp. 250 ff.
9. *Ibid.*, p. 282.

1962, reaching a total value of $532.8 million. Trade leveled off in 1963, but in 1964 increased at roughly the 1961 and 1962 rates, reaching $603.7 million.

TABLE I
DIRECTION OF FOREIGN TRADE
(value in millions of U.S. dollars)

			Exports to West Germany				
Country	*1958*	*1959*	*1960*	*1961*	*1962*	*1963*	*1964*
Czechoslovakia	49.4	56.3	61.7	62.0	65.9	65.4	72.1
Hungary	28.8	36.0	52.8	47.2	48.8	57.9	61.8
Poland	78.8	70.0	72.4	84.4	81.9	80.5	90.7
Rumania	22.4	16.4	35.7	52.3	61.8	52.9	61.3
Total	179.4	178.7	222.6	245.9	258.4	256.7	285.9

			Imports from West Germany				
Country	*1958*	*1959*	*1960*	*1961*	*1962*	*1963*	*1964*
Czechoslovakia	61.3	59.9	65.2	76.2	75.2	58.8	82.9
Hungary	30.5	42.4	44.5	50.8	49.5	63.2	73.8
Poland	71.0	81.1	76.2	69.1	65.6	65.4	78.4
Rumania	29.2	25.0	42.0	57.8	82.1	73.2	82.7
Total	192.0	208.4	232.9	253.9	272.4	260.6	317.8

Source: *Aussenhandel der Bundesrepublik Deutschland*, edited by Statistisches Bundesamt, Wiesbaden (Verlag W. Kohlhammer, Stuttgart/Mainz, 1958–64).

What were the political and economic motives behind this intensified trade? Which, political or economic, were the more decisive? Or is it that the economic situation in each of Germany's individual trading partners prompted it to search for new and more favorable trade agreements?

It is relatively easy to assess the political motives of the East European states. In Communist societies foreign trade is co-ordinated within an overall, centrally conceived policy framework. Social restlessness in Poland and the brutal oppression of the Hungarian revolt in 1956 had their impact on the policy formulation of most of the East European satellites. A major foreign policy objective of these states since 1956 has been to normalize political relations with the West. Foreign trade has served to further this end. Additionally, the East European states may have been prompted to increase trade with the West by the Soviet example itself, which has entailed more extra-bloc trade as an economic corollary to "peaceful coexistence." However, closer economic contacts with "capitalistic societies" could also be used to assert a degree of national independence from the Soviet Union. The Rumanian example is especially instructive.

In 1963 and 1964, Rumania expanded its political contact with the West considerably, with a view toward eventually diminishing its economic dependence on the USSR. In 1963, for the first time in eleven years, Rumanian audiences were permitted to hear without interference the Western radio programs of the Voice of America, Radio Free Europe and the BBC. This about-face was part of Rumania's general effort to cultivate a more cordial atmosphere with the West. The first step was soon followed by Rumania's offer to settle outstanding financial issues with Great Britain, France, West Germany, and the United States and Switzerland.

The Western powers responded promptly to Rumanian trade proposals. Whereas up to 1963 trade contracts with the West covered only secondary and minor industrial plants, from that year on Rumania sought and successfully concluded contracts affecting the main sectors of the economy. As early as 1964 in inviting Western business concerns to invest in Rumanian industry on the basis of a working partnership between Western capital and a Communist government Rumania put forward proposals unprecedented in the history of East-West trade since 1945. Rumanian officials offered guaranteed profits, protection against nationalization, and payment in hard currency.[10]

At the same time Rumania's resistance to Soviet economic plans stiffened, possibly because of a proposed "socialist division of labor" within the COMECON framework. Rumanian leaders regarded the proposal as a device to strengthen Moscow's

10. Michael Gamarnikov, "Eastern Partners for Western Businessmen," *East Europe*, Vol. XIV (September, 1965), p. 17.

economic pre-eminence, especially since it entailed significant curtailing of their country's drive to industrialize.[11]

Ideological considerations have also influenced Rumanian leadership. On April 16, 1964, *Scinteia*, one of the official party papers, pleaded for complete freedom of action of the competent organs in planning and executing exclusively Rumanian economic policies.[12] The publication of such a request by a party organ was not a trivial matter. It demonstrated on one hand an increasing national consciousness that is characteristic not only of Rumania but of Hungary and Poland as well, and to a lesser degree of Czechoslovakia. On the other hand, it clearly expressed the Rumanian leaders' reluctance to confer upon a supra-national authority certain functions which they chose to regard as belonging exclusively to the national domain.

Political Motivations

Although other East European states exercised more self-restraint than Rumania in their drive toward increased independence, by 1964 national considerations in Eastern Europe began to take precedence over the universalist claims of traditional Communism. West German leadership was sufficiently circumspect not to overemphasize the importance of these nationalist manifestations. First, the economies of the individual countries had been planned within the framework of COME-CON, which in the early 1960's held these states together more effectively than any other international body. Second, in 1964, 70 percent of the overall foreign trade of all the East European countries (with the exception of Yugoslavia) was in fact intra-COMECON trade. Clearly, the West German leadership could not realistically hope that a political breakthrough would necessarily follow from these economic developments.

In Germany prior to 1964, a wide variety of arguments were advanced in favor of extension of trade with East Europe. Those of private industrialist groups often appeared vague and utopian.

11. Press conference of Rumania's First Deputy Prime Minister Gheorghe Apostol in Vienna, July 7, 1964, *Presse und Informationsamt der Bundesrepublik* (Bonn, 1964).
12. "Meinungsverschiedenheiten im Ostblock," *Neue Zürcher Zeitung,* April 22, 1964.

There were certain groups which considered East-West trade a solid bridge between the two systems, indeed as the only bridge which could still connect the two halves of Europe. Other unofficial organizations entertained the hope that an active Eastern trade policy could ease the tribulations of Germany's division.[13] Another political argument in favor of more German trade with the East was that the extension of such trade would make the East European countries more dependent on the West in general and on Bonn in particular. It was hoped that growing economic dependence would stimulate the development of closer political contacts which eventually could result in political cooperation between the two systems.

The statements of government officials concerning the subject were less ambitious and more lucid. The first but rather general statement expressing the desire for improved German-East European relations came from Foreign Minister Gerhard Schröder in 1962 at the Party Convention of the Christian Democratic Union.[14] A year later Dr. Schröder restated the new orientation in more specific terms:

> We have recently carried on negotiations with the Polish government which went satisfactorily. The agreements recently concluded with the Polish government are the first steps . . . to re-establish official contacts with the states of Eastern Europe in order to ease the atmosphere and to further understanding of our mutual problems.[15]

In the same year Chancellor Erhard expressed the willingness of the Federal government to "increase and expand its economic exchanges with the Western European states."[16] And a

13. George Schröder, "Fühler nach dem Osten," *Die Welt*, November 26, 1964.
14. Dortmunder Parteitag der Christlich Demokratischen Union, *Rede des Herrn Aussenministers Dr. Gerhard Schröder* (Parteivorstand der CDU, Bonn, 1962).
15. Press Information Office of the German Federal Government, *Points of Main Emphasis in German Foreign Policy*, Address by Dr. Gerhard Schröder at the General Meeting of the Iron and Steel Industry Association in Düsseldorf, June 28, 1963 (Bonn, 1963).
16. News from the German Embassy, *Government Statement Made by Chancellor Ludwig Erhard in the Bundestag on October 18, 1963*.

few months later, in April 1964, Foreign Minister Schröder emphasized the importance of improving already existing trade relations between Bonn and East Europe by saying that "We wish to live in peace with our Eastern neighbors. That is why we . . . wish to trade with them . . . and to reestablish contacts that have been broken for so long."[17] Even at this early date the Federal government demonstrated West Germany's desire to use existing and prospective trade agreements and the establishment of official Trade Missions as a first step toward normalizing its political relations with the Eastern Bloc.

The first steps on the road toward normalization were taken by the establishment of the Federal Republic's official Trade Missions in Warsaw in 1963, and in Budapest, Bucharest, and Sofia in 1964. Did these missions fulfill Bonn's political expectations? Could such Trade Missions eventually be converted into permanent diplomatic posts with all the rights and privileges of such bodies? Was West German leadership, in circumventing the Hallstein Doctrine, signaling a willingness to be less dogmatic on such matters?

The Rumanian case demonstrated that Trade Missions could indeed serve as a stepping stone for normal diplomatic ties. After protracted negotiations West Germany and Rumania exchanged ambassadors in early 1967. This was the first breakthrough in West German-East European relations. Rumania is not comparable on a number of counts, however, to Poland or Czechoslovakia. Unlike the two other countries, Rumania has had no unsettled boundary problems with Germany, nor was it consistently following the Kremlin's foreign policy line. Furthermore, more than any of the other Communist countries of East Europe, Rumania has been quite willing to pursue an unorthodox foreign policy in the interests of rapid industrial development. Finally, Rumania's unique flexibility itself has enabled it to achieve certain political and economic objectives without real political concessions to West Germany.

"There is nothing more dangerous than to rely on doctrinair-

17. Press and Information Office of the German Federal Government, *Germany's Position and Germany's Future*, Address by Dr. Gerhard Schröder at the 11th Federal Congress of the Evangelical Circle of the CDU/CSU Parties, Munich, April 3, 1964 (Bonn, April 7, 1964).

ism in approaching foreign policy," said Foreign Minister Schröder in May, 1965, in a reference to the Hallstein Doctrine. On another occasion he stated explicitly that Bonn could establish diplomatic relations with all the East European states similar to those maintained with the USSR, regardless of existing theories and doctrines. Yet in disavowing the Hallstein Doctrine the Foreign Minister did not go as far as the leader of the Free Democratic Party, Erich Mende, who said flatly that the Doctrine could no longer be considered a useful instrument of German foreign policy.[18] However, the importance of these pronouncements was immediately weakened when Schröder himself insisted, in keeping with the Doctrine, that "it is only West Germany which has the right to be the sole representative of All Germany." This sort of cautious qualification is evidence that West Germany's new Eastern policy was still in its formative stages. These and similar statements injected a degree of ambiguity into Germany's policy toward East Europe.

Partly as a result of West German uncertainty as to exactly what the parameters of their new policy were, a number of specific problems arose. Poland, Hungary, and Bulgaria have demanded nothing less than the establishment of full diplomatic relations. From Bonn's point of view, this would impose upon them the impossibly premature abandonment of the Hallstein Doctrine and the eventual recognition of the East German regime. The compromise finally agreed upon was a curious example of the "art of the possible." It conferred upon the Trade Missions special privileges usually granted only to diplomatic missions while at the same time it restricted their freedom of political maneuver to what their name implied — trade.

More damaging than these structural shortcomings was the fact that the pronouncements of the West German politicians created the impression in East Europe that Bonn regarded its trade missions as bridges to full diplomatic relations. Although this impression was never explicitly discouraged by Bonn, the evident discrepancy between Dr. Schröder's allegedly pragmatic approach and Bonn's insistence on its claim to sole re-

18. "Europa endet nicht mehr an der Elbe," *Die Zeit*, July 9, 1965.

presentation became one of the greatest obstacles to the development of the desired normalization. Nor was the desire for normal relations onesided: for a variety of reasons all East European countries, in fact, desired fully accredited embassies and not substitutes. The Budapest Communist Party newspaper, *Népszabadság*, for instance, deplored that the establishment of Trade Missions in several Socialist states had not improved relations between these states and West Germany.[19] The Czechoslovak Deputy Foreign Minister Klicka stated that his country was more interested in normal relations with Bonn "than any other country in West Europe."[20] In addition there have been repeated attempts on Bonn's part to include in its trade agreements a stipulation that would officially recognize West Berlin as an integral part of the Federal Republic. Insistence on the inclusion of this stipulation has been one of the main stumbling blocks between Czechoslovakia and Bonn in their negotiations for the establishment and exchange of official trade missions.[21]

The hybrid character of the Trade Missions has been another obstacle toward normalization. The heads of the Missions have been highranking West German diplomats. The members of the Missions have enjoyed diplomatic immunity and customs privileges; yet, on the other hand, they have been prohibited from issuing visas or rendering protection to West German citizens. Worse, they have been unable to make political or even social contacts since they simply did not exist in the eyes of the respective Foreign Ministries. Bonn's "forerunners" have thus been operating in political and social isolation, with the benefit of diplomatic privilege but without diplomatic functions. Under such circumstances one could question whether substituting a halfhearted trade policy for formal diplomatic relations would ever lead to normalization.

Economic Motivations: East and West

The extension of trade has also been influenced by economic

19. *Népszabadság*, October 28, 1965.
20. Quoted in "Can Trade Replace Politics?" *Die Zeit*, November 5, 1965.
21. Alvin Münchmeyer, "Ausweitung des Osthandels — Aber wie?" *Aussenpolitik*, July, 1965, pp. 447–56. See also "Novotny Speaks," *East Europe*, December, 1965, p. 35.

motives on both sides of the Curtain. These economic considerations are easier to explain and to define than political motivations, which are often difficult to decipher and weigh.

The transition of all of the East European peoples from subjects to independent nations stretches over a period of approximately one hundred years. After the First World War all successor states to the Hapsburg, Romanoff, and Ottoman Empires
were predominantly agricultural societies, with the exception of
Czechoslovakia. Between the two Wars between 70 and 80
percent of the populations of Poland, Yugoslavia, Rumania,
and Bulgaria, and about 55 percent in Hungary, were engaged
in one way or another in agricultural enterprises. Agricultural
products were the basic source of national income, and they
also provided these countries with much-needed export commodities. Only Hungary and Czechoslovakia could export
significant quantities of finished and semi-finished industrial
products.

All of these East European countries were industrially underdeveloped, suffered from agricultural overpopulation, and were
characterized by a scarcity of capital investment funds. They
depended on the financial, technical, and technological in-
volvement of the West for developing their respective economies, and for solving their socio-political problems. Between
the Wars the West provided capital investment and technical
know-how, as well as exports of industrial products in exchange
for agricultural products and industrial raw material. This was
particularly true of Germany, with which these countries maintained the closest possible economic connections.

These patterns changed drastically after 1945. From this
time on the development of the economies of these states was
determined by two main factors. First, under Soviet aegis,
socio-political objectives basic to Communist ideology furnished
guidelines for redistribution of wealth immediately after the
war in East Europe. Second, Soviet financial and technical
assistance and Soviet organizational techniques inevitably had
a decisive effect on postwar economic development in this area.

After a relatively short transition period, uniform Communist
regimes, which severed economic ties with the West European
states, were established. A major turning point was the rejec-

tion of the Marshall Plan in 1948. The loss of close economic contacts with the West pushed the East European countries into the economic orbit of the Soviet Union, and these countries lost the small measure of economic independence they had enjoyed. Their economies were subordinated to the overall economic interests of the Soviet Union.

Soviet theory required that the East European countries accumulate a certain amount of capital, to ensure the transition of their weak agrarian economies to dynamic industrial economies. A centrally planned economic system and a state monopoly on foreign trade were considered indispensable tools for accomplishing this capital accumulation and the further development of "dynamic" industrial economies during the first stages after the take-off period. Such a transition, however, can be made only if the growth-rate and productive capacity of heavy industry (mining, iron, steel, machine, chemical industries) is kept extremely high, and in particular higher than the growth-rate of consumer goods industries.

In underdeveloped countries with unplanned economies, the demand for food and other consumers' commodities is somewhat elastic, and production surpluses may be used by the population itself. If this happens, surplus production which might otherwise be available for reinvestment is lost, and rapid development of the national economy is compromised. Consequently, according to Communist economic theorists, a high growth-rate can be reached only if production, prices and foreign trade are protected from the fluctuations of supply and demand of a market economy. To do this, a centrally planned economy, authoritarian price control, and state monopoly of foreign (and domestic) trade become necessary.

The application of this theory to Eastern Europe had two major results. One was the creation of heavy industrial complexes, carried out by means of all the pressure which the Party and the state were able to apply. The second was the complete destruction of the former agricultural system through sweeping land reforms followed by forced collectivization. One consequence of this economic policy was the absolute and relative decline of the agricultural sector of the economy. This very decline deprived each of the East European countries of their exportable agricultural surplus commodities. The loss of agricultural exports in turn seriously affected the balance of payments and the balance of trade, and caused the East European countries to import agricultural products on a large scale.

Nevertheless, in a relatively short period of time, the East European nations transformed themselves from mainly agricultural and raw material export communities into agricultural-industrial economies. The result of this successful transition — brought about at a tremendously high cost, and by an almost systematic lowering of the standard of living — was that around 1956–7 the bulk of the national income of the East European countries was provided by the industrial sector of their economies. Moreover, the utilization of the productive capacity of their infant industries brought about an expansion of domestic production. This development is partially responsible for favorable response of the East European states to West German economic overtures.

Beginning in about 1956–7 this need for expanded trade relations necessitated a more realistic economic policy in East Europe. At that time, attempts to coordinate domestic production with foreign trade were begun, and they have continued over the last ten to twelve years. These developments have paved the way for intensified trade relations with the West.

The original function of Western imports in East Europe was merely to fill the gaps in domestic production which had resulted from faulty economic planning: the amount of commodities imported was set by the plans, and the volume of exports was kept equal to imports. Foreign trade thus served a twofold purpose. Importing was confined to commodities that either could not be produced domestically or that could be produced only at prohibitive costs. At the same time, exports provided the countries with the much-needed foreign exchange to pay for their imports, or to clear their formerly accumulated debts.

However, greater industrialization and an increasing demand for consumer goods made it imperative to modify the rigidly doctrinaire approach to economics. Some shortcomings of centralized planning were recognized as early as 1953, as indicated by the introduction of a modified New Economic Policy in most of the satellite countries immediately following

Stalin's death.[22] But the frustrations and failures of Communist economic planning continued for another decade while economists all over the Eastern bloc slowly discovered the magnitude of the problems which could be caused by severely restricting imports of badly needed commodities as well as consumer goods. Demand for both types of goods increased steadily from the early 1960's. Simultaneously, rapidly increasing industrial output prompted these countries to search for new markets. Although there is a safety valve built into COMECON insofar as it provides member countries with a market for their products, the buying capacity of this market is limited. It is the West, and especially West Germany, that provides a natural market for East European products.

Aside from tacit submission to the iron law of supply and demand, three other factors may have contributed to the expansion of trade with the West. Immediately after the establishment of the European Economic Community the Kremlin predicted its ultimate failure. This prophecy did not come true, but the robust success of the Common Market and the constantly rising living standards in all member countries had an important impact on the Eastern Bloc. Secondly, East Europe was impressed by the high quality of the Western products. Finally, the exploitative price policies of the Soviet Union may also have influenced the planners of satellite economies in their quest for intensified trade with the West.

Under bilateral trade agreements concluded up to 1964-5 the satellite states committed themselves to deliver industrial products to the Soviet Union at prices 20 to 30 percent below the world market price. Dr. Erich Apel, Chairman of the Planning Commission of the German Democratic Republic, committed suicide because of the impossible choices with which this exploitation faced him. From 1965 on the Soviet Union raised the prices of its imports from the former satellites to about 10 to 15 percent below the world market prices. By 1965, the East European states had concluded trade agreements with Moscow for a plan-period of 1966–70.[23] According to the avail-

22. Godfrey Lias, "Satellite States in the Post-Stalin Era," *International Affairs*, London, January, 1954.
23. For detailed information see *Yearbook of International Statistics*, Years 1964–1966, United Nations Publication (New York, 1964, 1966).

able information,[24] there has been a definite upward trend in trade within the bloc, and an accelerated increase was planned for 1966–70. However, it is important to emphasize that this proposed increase (the result of economic consultations in the winter of 1964–5) has been necessitated by practical considerations such as foreign exchange shortage, or in many cases the dependence of the East European countries on Soviet oil and its by-products. Political considerations, as demonstrated by the case of Rumania, have been playing an ever-diminishing role.

West Germany's economic motives in expanding East-West trade were simple. Supply and demand, the basic governing forces in Western economic systems, have played a decisive role. The opportunities offered by a consumers' market of some 300 million people were immense. By 1964, it was obvious that demand in East Europe for industrial and for consumer goods was relatively high and would remain so in the future. Two additional economic factors could also have played a major role in German decision-making. First, beginning in 1962 competition among West European states for this market was rather keen, since the foreign trade policies of the EEC countries were not coordinated at that time. A second factor which undoubtedly prompted West Germans to make deliberate efforts to increase their trade with the East European countries was the clearly discernible decline in the volume of Germany's *overall* trade with the Communist bloc during 1962–3, as indicated in Table II.

The decline in the exchange of commodities between West Germany and the Communist bloc amounted to $38.7 million in imports and to $66.2 million in exports; it had also been accompanied by a serious $27.5 million debit balance in West Germany's overall trade. The debit balance was less the result of an increase in the volume of imports to West Germany than of a decline in West German exports, especially to the Soviet Union.

A number of explanations for this absolute and relative decline in West Germany's trade with the Eastern bloc suggest

24. *Ibid.* See also *Népszabadság*, April 30, 1965, and *Statistical Pocketbook of the German Democratic Republic 1966*, Foreign Trade Section, pp. 121–30, *Staatsverlag der Deutschen Demokratischen Republik* (Berlin, 1966).

TABLE II

Country	Imports to West Germany		Exports from West Germany	
	(in millions of U.S. dollars)			
	1962	*1963*	*1962*	*1963*
Soviet Union	214.4	208.8	206.5	153.5
Czechoslovakia	65.9	65.4	75.2	58.8
Poland	81.9	80.5	65.6	65.4
Hungary	48.8	57.9	49.5	63.2
Rumania	61.8	52.9	82.1	73.2
Bulgaria	61.4	29.4	24.5	23.5
Albania	0.4	0.2	0.5	0.7
North Korea North Vietnam Mongolia	0.7	0.8	1.0	0.4
Total	534.6	495.9	504.9	438.7

Source: *Aussenhandel der Bundesrepublik Deutschland*, edited by Statistisches Bundesamt, Wiesbaden (Verlag Kohlhammer, Stuttgart/Mainz, 1962–3).

themselves. First, since 1963 the Russians had had difficulty financing their imports from West Germany because they were compelled at this time to set aside foreign exchange for large-scale wheat purchases in the West. In addition, West Germany honored the embargo on pipelines, which resulted in approximately a 60 percent reduction of her exports of iron and steel. Furthermore, some of the goods exported by the East European trading partners had been difficult to place on the West German market because they were of poor quality. On the other hand, however, the agricultural policies of the Common Market countries also made the import of some agricultural products (pork, poultry, etc.) extremely difficult, especially for Poland and Hungary. Finally, the West German government hesitated to extend long-term credits, badly needed by all of the East European countries and this undoubtedly also contributed to the temporary decline of trade. The fact that other NATO and EEC countries offered government-secured long-term credits, and began to compete in earnest for the East European market induced the West German government to extend up to three and four years of credit to Poland, Hungary, Rumania, and Bulgaria in 1964 and in 1965.[25]

German economic enterprises in East Europe have been relatively successful. In 1965, the Hungarian Ministry for Forestry and Metallurgy in cooperation with the Ministry for Foreign Trade jointly established a Bureau of Technical Cooperation and Foreign Trade. As early as March, 1965, the director of this Bureau declared that "technical cooperation in the future between Hungary and West Germany is the only realistic approach toward further improvement in the volume of trade between the two countries."[26] In this article Dr. Sándor Cséky listed six main fields of eventual cooperation, ranging from production of machines and complete industrial plants in Hungary under West German technical direction to joint marketing policies. The proposal also envisaged a continuous exchange of specialists, joint planning and exchange of blueprints. Most far-reaching was Dr. Cséky's call for uninhibited joint research and development to new methods in production, and for coordinated action in the investment policy of the firms involved. This type of close cooperation is seldom found even among firms in the Western societies.

Economic and political obstacles notwithstanding, a number of agreements were concluded in 1965-6 between German firms on the one hand, and Polish, Hungarian and other East European enterprises on the other. For instance, an agreement on economic cooperation between the Rheinische Stahlwerke AG, Essen, and Hungary, or the plan for a pipeline factory by Krupp or Mannesmann in Csepel have been of the utmost importance. These agreements demonstrated the possibilities for further trade expansion to West German political leadership. Also, the increasing willingness of the East European countries to experiment with unorthodox trade relations showed that traditional Communist practices had to be supplemented in order to rationalize and develop export production and thereby to increase hard currency income.

25. Hermann Gross, "Wirtschaftssyteme und Wirtschaftspolitik der südosteuropäischen Staaten," *Südost Europa Jahrbuch*, Vol. 7, pp. 1-11 (München, 1966).
26. "Sondernummer: Ungarn," *Industriekurier*, March 8, 1965.

Political Impact of Trade in Eastern Europe

Expanded German and Western trade relations had a great impact on Eastern Europe. The intensification of this trade and the concomitant need for improved quality production have been among the factors which led to the partial and cautious decentralization of East European economies. Decentralization, in turn, created a good deal of uneasiness among the Party *aparatchiki*, however. The influence of the old-timers in the Communist Parties has been so great that, although the plans for decentralization were drafted in 1965, they were put into effect in Czechoslovakia only in 1967, and Hungary did not even begin to implement them until 1968. Finally, since all Communist countries found it expedient to export as much as possible to the West, the East European countries began to compete with each other in the West European markets.

Trade intensification has also caused ideological problems for Communist leaders. Polish leadership has had obvious difficulties explaining the proposed establishment of a joint Krupp-Polish enterprise. As envisaged, the enterprise was to function on a purely capitalistic basis.[27] Polish ideologists had the unenviable task of convincing their Party cadres (and presumably fraternal parties in East Europe) that there was no inconsistency between Communist ideology and cooperation in a capitalist enterprise.

Another result of the Western economic invasion was a controversy in Hungary concerning the real or imagined political disadvantages of extended trade. Party leaders and leading economists betrayed a certain nervousness about the new policies:

> The most important characteristic of the new tactics of imperialists is that they hope to play the individual states of the Socialist camp against the Soviet Union. The imperialists attempt to exacerbate the remnants of nationalism in our camp . . . and to place emphasis on our economic difficulties. [They] hope to deal with us one by one so that the political and economic structure of our respective

27. "Noch ist Poland nicht gewonnen," *Die Welt*, November, 25, 1964.

countries will be shifted to the right and will be liberalized in the Western style.[28]

This passage said a great deal. First, the Hungarian Party admitted that the new West European and German effort to expand trade with the East could be successful. Second, the reference to "remnants of nationalism" implicitly confessed how dangerous a force nationalism is still feared to be within the Communist camp. Finally, the reference to liberalization indicated a certain fear of this process.

It has often been argued in the West that there will eventually be a significant liberalization of political and economic structures in Eastern Europe. Some Communist leaders have understandably been at pains to take issue with this view. In 1963, János Kádár stated that "what the West considers as liberalization is nothing else but the conscientious and consistently pursued desire of the Party and that of the system of the People's Democracy."[29] Two years later the Prime Minister of Hungary, Gyula Kállay, speaking to Parliament, emphasized the dangerous influences of Western contacts on the "development of socialist morality,"[30] a sign that Communist leadership in Hungary had become apprehensive. Nor, in point of fact, has the "process of liberalization" taken the course hoped for by the West in Rumania, for example. Although during the last few years Rumania has had extensive economic contacts with the West, and has demonstrated in its foreign policy a surprisingly high degree of independence from the Soviet Union, the alleged "process of liberalization" has shown much less progress in Rumania than in Hungary.

In spite of some nervous fluctuation, West German-East European trade from 1964 on shows an upward curve. Since March, 1965, credits of up to five years and in specific cases of up to eight years have been extended to most East European states. This credit policy was further liberalized in March, 1966.[31] There was a considerable increase in West Germany's

28. *Népszabadság*, February 24, 1965.
29. *Ibid.*, December 24, 1965.
30. "Ostblock verstärkt Angriffe auf Bonn," *Die Welt*, October 15, 1965; also see *Magyar Hirek*, December, 1965.
31. Gross, *op. cit.*, p. 5.

exports to East Europe in 1964. Similarly, the liberal approach toward credit policy increased East European exports to West Germany in the years of 1965–6, as seen in Table III.

TABLE III

Country	Exports to West Germany		Imports from West Germany	
		(value in millions of U.S. dollars)		
	1965	*1966* (*Jan–June*)	*1965*	*1966* (*Jan–June*)
Czechoslovakia	84.1	40.2	100.5	48.7
Poland	108.9	48.9	91.5	42.5
Rumania	72.4	35.5	115.6	51.1
Hungary	71.9	33.4	76.7	47.1

Source: *Der Aussenhandel der Bundesrepublik Deutschland*, T1: *Zusammenfassende Übersichten, 1965*, and January–June 1966. Edited by Statistisches Bundesamt, Wiesbaden.

Although at the time of this writing 1966 figures were available for January–June only, they indicated a strong upward trend, and the increase in volume of trade has in fact continued.

The economic and political motivations for increased trade taken together present a fascinating picture. Both in West Germany and in the East European countries political and economic motives were closely interwoven. It is true that the East European countries provide West Germany with a large market, and that Bonn has been eager to avail itself of this opportunity for increased trade. But it is also true that West Germany's trade with the East European countries represented only some 5 percent of her total volume of trade at this time. Moreover, West Germany has imported commodities from Poland, Hungary, and Rumania which she herself produces or to which she has easy access.[32] These facts suggest that, in expanding her trade to the East, West German leadership has been influenced more by political motives than by economic considerations.

32. Indicated by Foreign Minister Schröder in *Points of Emphasis, op. cit.*, p. 3.

The opposite is the case with the East European countries. A flat 35 percent of all of the imported commodities from the West (20 percent of which are from West Germany) consisted of production and capital investment commodities: machines, heavy industrial equipment, iron and steel products, and chemicals. All these items are badly needed for further development of the national economies of these countries. Moreover, such commodities are not available, or can be obtained only in insufficient quantity and of unsatisfactory quality within the Communist bloc. Acquiring high-quality producers' goods was without a doubt a major incentive for the East European countries to intensify their trade relations with West Germany.

Bonn's primary political aim behind this cautious economic offensive has been to end West Germany's political isolation from its Eastern neighbors. It was also hoped that re-establishing prewar economic contacts would pave the way for a politically more conciliatory attitude on the part of the East European states. The results have been modest. Establishment of joint companies, favorable trade agreements and extended credits have not basically altered the political prejudice and attitudes of the East European countries. It is true that Bonn succeeded in establishing normal diplomatic relations with Rumania early in 1967, and in concluding a trade agreement accompanied by an exchange of Trade Missions with Czechoslovakia in July of the same year. But their achievements have been of little political value so far.

West Germany's problems in establishing economic ties with her Eastern neighbors have been primarily non-economic. The most important political factor in the area was and remains the Soviet Union. The Soviet Union's dominating position has allowed it to exercise decisive political influence over East Europe.

In 1967 another fundamentally important political factor was the ambiguity of the German *Ostpolitik* itself. On one hand, Bonn has adopted a more flexible approach toward diplomatic relations and related problems. On the other, the Hallstein Doctrine had not been officially repudiated. Disagreement within West Germany's governing party over basic principles of *Ostpolitik* have been clearly visible from 1965 on, and this has contributed to confusion at home and abroad. Foreign Minister Schröder, presumably supported by the northern, Protestant faction of the Christian Democratic Union, has advocated a more conciliatory policy toward the East. Former Defense Minister Franz Joseph Strauss, Freiherr von Guttenberg, and the clerical wing of the Christian Socialist Union have taken a much harder line and have vigorously opposed any policy of relaxation. Former Chancellor Adenauer supported them until 1965, and his enormous prestige provided them with considerable support. Lack of consensus within the governing party — as well as within the opposition — has severely limited the political leadership's freedom of action. Moreover, it has jeopardized the credibility of the Erhard government in the eyes of the East European countries.

A third political factor has been until recently, the unsolved problem of Germany's eastern boundaries. In 1964, Chancellor Erhard repudiated the 1938 settlement, thus attempting to reassure Czechoslovakia with respect to the Sudetenland. But this more or less unequivocal repudiation aroused political opposition in Bonn, and has stiffened the resistance of the Czechs toward West German overtures. More than anything else, the unsettled question of the Oder-Neisse border and the eastern territories impaired even a partial reconciliation between Poland and West Germany, and delayed the formulation of a new, viable, *Ostpolitik*. The political role of these and related territorial problems will be discussed in depth in the following chapters.

2

the quest for
a new consensus

By 1965 both West German politicians and politically aware sectors of the population had come to realize that the Eastern policy had reached an apparent impasse. During the last two years Bonn had, it was true, been able to re-establish and to expand its economic relations with most East European countries. But through mutual exchange of Trade Missions the Federal Republic had created an ambiguous diplomatic presence in these countries. Neither the abundant flow of commodities in both directions, nor the presence of Trade Missions of uncertain political status had provided the Germans and their East European neighbors with a point of departure from which there could be progress toward ultimate reconciliation.

The Erhard-Schröder period (1963–6) could claim only meager success in its policy toward Eastern Europe in comparison to the Adenauer era. At the same time friendship and cooperation between Paris and Bonn was reduced to an alarming minimum, a fact which cannot be attributed exclusively to de Gaulle's political extravagances. Insistence on co-possession of nuclear weapons within NATO, or at least on participation in nuclear strategic planning, raised questions about Bonn's motives, even among the Western partners. Unrealistic as they were, these publicly-proclaimed policy objectives provided the East with an invaluable propaganda weapon.

The greatest political mistake of the Erhard era was made by default: failure to formulate a clear-cut policy toward East Europe and toward the German problem. The Erhard government hesitated a long time over whether to abandon the Hallstein Doctrine, and this automatically postponed the question of normalizing Bonn's diplomatic relations with East Europe. Another mistake was that the post-Adenauer government would not take any *initiative* toward the solution of Germany's national problem. Finally, insisting on the "legal validity" of the 1937 frontiers and upholding the right of Sudeten Germans to their former homeland, while at the same time paradoxically repudiating the Munich Agreement, the Erhard government actually deepened the rift between Germany and her Eastern neighbors.

By mid-1965 there were also indications that West Germany's Eastern policy as it had evolved was not well thought of in a society which, having solved most of its pressing domestic political and economic problems, had turned with increasing interest toward its unsolved national problem. A public opinion poll taken as early as October, 1963, showed that only 34 percent of the electorate wanted Adenauer's overall foreign policies to be continued by his successor. Another 44 percent opted for a change in policy, and the rest was undecided.[1] A different poll which had been taken periodically since 1951 showed growing concern with reunification and with unsettled relations with Poland and Czechoslovakia.[2] In 1951 only 18 percent of a cross section of the population considered the question of reunification the most important general question for Germany, but this percentage rose by 1965 to an all-time high of 47 percent. In both polls the question of *Ostpolitik* was

1. *Soll die Politik Adenauers fortgesetzt werden?* (Pressedienst, Institut für Demoskopie, Allensbach, Allensbach, 1963), pp. 2–3.
2. *Wiedervereinigung: Grösstes Anliegen der jungen Generation* (Pressedienst, Institut für Demoskopie Allensbach, Allensbach, 1965); noteworthy is the fact that in 1965 persons in the age group 16–29, i.e. a group which does not have any reminiscences about a united Germany, did consider the question of reunification as the most important *general* problem for West Germany.

included, and the response was as high as 54 percent in favor of a more active policy toward Eastern Europe.

It is safe to say, without exaggerating the reliability of public opinion polls, that the above data do accurately reflect broad changes in the attitude of West Germany's population toward the question of reunification in general and toward a more active policy *vis-à-vis* West Germany's Eastern neighbors in particular. By the mid-sixties, then, there was a fundamental discrepancy between the population's preferences and the government's foreign policy. As a leading foreign political commentator said,[3] there was in 1965 no clear-cut West German idea for a solution of the German problem within the framework of a peace settlement acceptable to the world, nor was there an imaginative policy for a transition period in which the national identity in both parts would be preserved and the division of the country made bearable.

Public Debate: The Evangelical Church

In our century, foreign policy is not an occult science. It is no longer the refined and exclusive chess game of a few professional and privileged diplomats, as it was in the 18th century when the results of the diplomatic game were accepted by the population with astonishment or indifference. The time is past in Germany when Bismarck could persist in a foreign policy which flew in the face of outraged public opinion.[4] In democratic societies of the 20th century, and especially in postwar West Germany, the formulation and execution of long-range foreign policy must be based on a rather broad consensus. If it is not, the initiative for reformulation of policy will come either from the leadership itself, or if the leadership is unable or unwilling to undertake the task, from non-governmental circles.

In the second half of 1965 public debate over the formulation of an all-Germany policy (*Deutschlandpolitik*) was in full swing. It began with the Memorandum of the Evangelical Church in

3. Theo Sommer, "Denken an Deutschland ," *Die Zeit*, March 14, 1966, p. 1
4. The author refers here to the period *before* 1870–71 when Bismarck's forceful attempts at Germany's unification under Prussian rule were very much resented by such states as Bavaria, Hesse, Würtemberg, Baden, etc.

Germany.[5] On October 1, 1965, the Council of the Evangelical Church (*Rat der Evangelischen Kirche in Deutschland*) permitted the publication of a Memorandum composed by the Chamber for Public Responsibility of the Church under the chairmanship of Professor Ludwig Raiser at the University of Tübingen. The paper was presented to the public on October 14. Even within the Church itself the Memorandum met with a rather mixed reaction.

The Memorandum was most vigorously opposed by those refugees from the lands incorporated into Poland organized in the *Bund der Vertriebenen* (League of Expellees). In its first declaration the Bund described the Memorandum as a "striking example of that dilettantism with which politics are made in the Bundesrepublik."[6] It further said that the Church had misused its privileged position by attempting to undermine the legal basis of West Germany in the question of the lost territories in the East. In another declaration, issued by the Council of the Representatives of East German Territories under the chairmanship of Philippe von Bismarck, the Memorandum was branded highly dangerous because "it falsifies the conceptual basis of Bonn's *Ostpolitik*, which rests on a consensus between the government, the political parties, and the representatives of the millions of expelled Germans."[7] Less than a week after these two declarations, the Presidium of the *Bund* issued a resolution protesting the Memorandum of the Evangelical Church, describing it, *inter alia*, as "morally, historically, legally and politically irresponsible."[8]

In addition to the not entirely unexpected attitude of the League of Expellees, the German press reacted to the Memorandum with an unusual degree of skepticism. What made this

5. *Denkschrift der Evangelischen Kirche in Deutschland über die Lage der Vertriebenen und das Verhältnis des deutschen Volkes zu seinen östlichen Nachbarn* (Verlag des Amtsblattes der Evangelischen Kirche in Deutschland, Hanover, 1965).
6. "Vertriebene protestieren gegen EKD-Denkschrift," *Die Welt*, October 17, 1965, p. 2; see also Bernt Conrad, "Die Grenzen im Osten," editorial in *Die Welt*, October 19, 1965, pp. 1–2.
7. *Erklärung des Rates der Ostdeutschen Landesvertretungen* (Rat der ostdeutschen Landesvertretungen, Hamburg, 1965).
8. "Vertriebene . . . ," *op. cit.*, see also *Bemühungen der evangelischen und katholischen Kirche um eine Aussöhnung zwischen Deutschland un Polen*, Europa Archiv, Vol. XXL, No. 1 Dokumente, p. D1 ff.

Memorandum so unacceptable? It did not advise the government to repudiate officially the right of the expellees to their former homes. It did not advocate the renunciation of the 1937 frontiers. It did not even declare the infamous Munich Agreement as null and void.

The authors of the Memorandum, a political document *par excellence*, did not deviate from official formulas concerning the cession of former German territories to Poland. In saying that ". . . the temporary decisions of the August 2, 1945, Potsdam Protocols . . . have still not been replaced, nor have they been legalized by a final international settlement," the authors adopt the official view that the status of the territories East of the Oder-Neisse border was not yet settled.[9] Nor did the authors choose to dispute the justice of the expellees' claim to their former homeland. The statement saying that "under the prevailing principles of international law the mass expulsion and forceful deportation of large segments of the population by a state which occupies the territory of another is an illegal act,"[10] various references to the Charter of the United Nations and to the Geneva Agreement of 1940 concerning the protection of the civilian population in wartimes, clearly indicate that the authors of the Memorandum did not disassociate themselves from the government's and the expellees' official concepts in this matter. In addition, the document discussed at length the legal aspects of Poland's right to the former German territories, actually echoing the official attitude toward this problem as it was represented from Adenauer to Erhard.

Legal arguments have occupied a prominent position in discussions of the German problem. This has been true of debate both within West Germany and internationally, and so the authors of the Memorandum were in a sense obliged to deal with the legal aspects of the problem. The crux of the question turns, of course, on the fact that Poland and the Soviet Union contend the incorporation and subsequent administration of former German territories as final and legally unassailable, whereas the government of the Federal Republic considers this arrangement temporary and thus subject to change as part of

9. Denkschrift, *op. cit.*, p. 4.
10. *Ibid.*, p. 18.

the terms of a final peace settlement. Two questions posed by the Church's Memorandum identify its point of departure in legal matters involving the German-Polish problem: "Has the transfer of sovereignty in Germany's former Eastern territories become already final?" and "Was the expulsion of the original German population from these territories in accord with the principles of international law?"[11]

The Memorandum answered both of these questions in the negative. In discussing the first, it referred to the Four Power agreement at the Potsdam Conference and to the Paris and London Protocols of 1954 regulating the relationship between the former Occupying Powers and Western Germany, emphasizing that both documents have subjected the issue of the former German territories to a final peace settlement.[12] The Memorandum further referred to established principles of international law which prohibit the unilateral annexation of territories, and it stated that "the act of unconditional surrender of the Third Reich did not destroy the state itself, consequently German sovereignty over the territories beyond the Oder-Neisse line was never abolished."[13] The conclusion drawn from this reasoning is that "if it is Poland's desire to retain the territories it has occupied since 1945 . . . it [Poland] needs a legal act which will legitimize this desire."[14] However, the argument continued, "this act can be legalized only by the consent of Germany."

As these passages from the much-debated Memorandum show, there is no difference in principle between the Church's approach and that of West German policymakers. What made the Memorandum a unique document was that, unlike the pronouncements of the West German leadership, it took discussion of the German-Polish issue beyond the legal arguments. While the Memorandum accepted the validity of the legal claims on which West Germany's policy toward Poland had been based, it also warned against their indiscriminate political application, because "it may jeopardize the process of recon-

11. *Ibid.*, p. 21.
12. *Ibid.*, p. 24.
13. *Loc. cit.*
14. *Ibid.*, p. 25.

ciliation, which has to precede any political act, between the two countries."

The Evangelical Church approached the problem from two perspectives, moral and political. With regard to moral issues, it accepted German guilt for Poland's sufferings prior to and during World War II. Then the Memorandum poses a fundamental question: whether or not it is morally permissible to aim at the complete *re-establishment* of German sovereignty beyond the Oder-Neisse line. No such question had ever been asked by so politically influential a non-political body in Germany before; but by 1965 it had become evident that if West Germany honestly desired reconciliation with its Eastern neighbors, such questions had to be asked and answered.

Even more important than the Evangelical Church's approach to moral issues was its approach to the political. The basis of its political approach was that in the future Germany will have to respect not only the right of the Polish people to exist but also "the space within which the Polish state can further develop."[15] This statement was central. Not only did it acknowledge the wrongs done to the Polish people from Frederick the Great to Hitler, but it also, however implicitly, recognized that Poland has some rights to former German territories. It further stated that possession of territories formerly belonging to Germany "has become a vital economic necessity for Poland,"[16] especially since the cession of Polish territories to the Soviet Union, for which the Third Reich was mainly responsible. Carrying this line of reasoning one step further, the Church, while recognizing that the mere passage of time could not in and of itself give Poland legal title over these territories, did recognize the importance of the time factor. First, it acknowledged that Poland has been relatively successful in integrating the questioned territories into the social and political structure of the Polish state. Secondly, it realized that whereas a *restitutio in integrum* may have been possible in 1945 or 1946, "twenty years after the War this would be unthinkable." In this connection, the Memorandum emphasized Poland's need for security and its right, in the light of its

15. *Ibid.*, p. 22.
16. *Ibid.*, p. 24.

historical experience with Germany, to choose its own boundaries; it further asserted that this right will have to be respected by Germany. Finally, in advocating a mutual conciliatory
attitude toward the problem, the Memorandum concluded that
"insistence on legal points of view by both sides will not solve
the conflict. Consequently a compromise must be sought which
will establish the basis of a new coexistence between the Polish
and the German peoples."[17]

The importance of the Evangelical Church's bold initiative
should not be underestimated. The Evangelical Church represents the second largest denominational group in West
Germany and its statement, though couched in cautiously
chosen terms, was taken seriously.

By 1965 there were other indications of increasing demand
for a rethinking of West German foreign policy. Among the
signs of disenchantment were the publication of the very unorthodox study, *Reform der Deutschlandpolitik*, by Wilhelm Wolfgang Schuetz,[18] the chairman of the Kuratorium for Indivisible
Germany on the one hand, along with many other significant
contributions on the other. Even more significantly, in August,
1965, 54 percent of West Germany's population — including
West Berlin — envisaged a future Germany reunited but without the lost territories of East Prussia, Pomerania, and Silesia.[19]
Not only did the poll indicate that an absolute majority of the
West German population expected eventually to accept a
Germany with final territorial losses, but it also suggested that
such losses could be accepted without overwhelming national
resentment.

The Memorandum of the Evangelical Church in Germany

17. *Loc. cit.*
18. Wilhelm Wolfgang Schuetz, *Reform der Deutschlandpolitik* (Kuratorium
Unteilbares Deutschland, 1965), *passim.*
19. According to the findings of the Institut für Demoskopie Allensbach, a
cross section of the West German population, including West Berlin, was
asked the following questions, "In what way do you envisage a reunited
Germany? Do you think of the unification of the Federal Republic and the
Soviet Zone (East Germany) only, or do you envisage a Germany which
will also include East Prussia, Pomerania, and Silesia?"; 54 percent
preferred the unification of West and East Germany, and only 34 percent
opted for a Germany within its 1937 boundaries. The rest were either
undecided or had no opinion.

was thus a major milestone in post-World War II German history. It confronted squarely the question: could and should Bonn take the initiative in formulating an entirely new Eastern policy? It acknowledged the importance of twenty years within existing boundaries for Poland and Germany alike and therefore recognized the importance of political considerations instead of legal ones. The Memorandum in effect took present-day political realities as its point of departure. In conceding that the Polish-administered territories are of vital interest to the Polish people, the Evangelical Church made a bold attempt at eliminating one of the many stumbling blocks in Polish-German relations. Finally, in stating all these in rather unequivocal terms, the Memorandum was promulgated for two important purposes. The first of these was an earnest effort to replace the political and emotional taboos of the Cold War by providing the German public with a new set of political reference points. Secondly, the Church in search for the lowest common denominator, not between the two governments but between the *Polish and German nations*, made the first conciliatory step by a major West German institution toward Poland since the end of World War II. This attempt to initiate some sort of grass roots reconciliation was not made in vain, for it was followed by an unprecedented exchange of letters between the Polish and German Catholic bishops. This event revealed a deep desire for normalization within the two nations, but it further demonstrated the intransigence of Poland's communist government on this issue.

Public Debate: The Polish and German Catholic Bishops

On November 18, 1965, shortly before the dismissal of the Ecumenical Council in Rome, the Catholic bishops of Poland delivered a letter to their German colleagues inviting them to participate in the celebration of the millennium of Poland's Christianization.[20] The letter was motivated by the ecumenical

20. *Einladung zur Teilnahme an der Tausendjahrfeier der Christianisierung Polens in Tschenstochau im Jahre 1966*, Katholische Nachrichtenagentur, Dokumentation Nr. 34, December 5, 1965, p. 14. See also *German-Polish Dialogue* (Atlantic Forum, Bonn, Brussels, New York, 1966), which contains the full text of the letter exchange along with statements and comments of the international press.

spirit which prevailed in Rome at that time and was much more than a simple invitation. It was a genuine and urgent appeal to the two nations for their reconciliation. By recapitulating the history of Polish-German relations throughout the centuries and thus placing the seemingly hopeless present into historical perspective, the Polish bishops' invitation touched directly on the very heart of the problem.

Because they realized that the differences between Poland and Germany are essentially political and that solutions would ultimately depend upon the politicians, the Polish bishops chose to discuss the problem in its moral dimension. There is no trace of Polish nationalism as practiced by the Gomulka regime in the letter — nationalism from which the Polish Church has not been free either. The Polish Church fathers deny that the "possession of former German territories is a question of survival for the Polish nation."[21] However, neither did they claim that the former German territories in the East now under Polish administration are Polish territories that have been rightfully returned to the Polish Nation. "We will understand," the letter says, "that the Polish Western border on the Oder and Neisse is, for Germany, a bitter fruit of the last war." But, the letter continues, "Where else could have the millions of Poles gone who were also expelled from Polish eastern territories?"[22]

The final part of the letter contained one of the most important messages conveyed to the German people since 1945. In speaking about the suffering of the millions of German refugees and expellees, the bishops acknowledged the wrongs done to the German people, and implicitly accepted moral responsibility themselves. They further acknowledged the existence, activity, and subsequent persecution of those Germans who during the Third Reich belonged to the "other Germany", thus repudiating the theory of collective German guilt. The

21. *Ibid.*, p. 15.
22. *Loc. cit.* For the sake of accuracy, however, it should be emphasized that the population of the Polish Eastern territories was largely non-Polish who remained in the Soviet Union. It should also be pointed out that the number of expelled Germans exceeded the number of those Poles who moved westward. To this see: Hansjacob Stehle, *The Independent Satellite: Society and Politics in Poland Since 1945* (Frederick A. Praeger, New York, 1965), pp. 271 ff.

Polish message was the first of this kind which had come from behind the Iron Curtain; and, moreover, the message came from the country that had suffered the most from Nazi Germany. "These are words," as one of the leading German journals pointed out, "at which the German people, twenty years after the War, grasp as a drowning man grasps at the saving rope."[23]

The Polish bishops went further than simple recognition of German suffering. The following sentences are the pith of the message: ". . . let us try to forget! No more polemics, no more Cold War, but rather the beginning of a dialogue . . . in spite of everything, in spite of hot irons between the two nations."[24] These words were not empty rhetoric, neither were they an inappropriate political initiative as the Polish government claimed. One-fourth of the Polish episcopate perished in concentration camps during the Nazi occupation, and more than two thousand priests were either executed by the Nazis, or lost their lives during the War. The sincerity of the Polish bishops asking for and granting forgiveness, and thus seeking a reconciliation between the two nations, is above question.

Ever since the end of the Second World War, the Polish-German dialogue — insofar as Poland spoke with her own voice and not with that of Moscow — had been a veritable dialogue of the deaf. It is not Communist ideology or differences in respective politico-economic structures only that separate the two nations and militate against national political discussion. The arguing of this problem must be sought elsewhere. The fact that over one-fifth of the Polish nation fell victim to Nazi Germany's criminal war policy caused understandable bitterness on one side — while the subsequent rather successful "polonization" of Silesia and large parts of East Prussia which began with the expulsion of millions of Germans from a territory which they had inhabited for centuries provided just such a wellspring of bitterness on the other. The situation was further exacerbated by the refusal of most expellees and of West Germany itself (where the majority sought asylum) to formulate a foreign policy based on the de facto existence of the Oder-

23. Hans Zehrer, "Die polnischen Bischoefe," *Die Welt*, December 4, 1965, pp. 1–2.
24. Denkschrift, *op. cit.*, p. 20.

Neisse border. This in turn raised the spectre of a new German revanchism which, rightly or wrongly, has haunted Poland ever since the early fifties. Germans and Slavs had coexisted for hundreds of years, but in the aftermath of the Second World War, both sides distorted the whole history of the two nations by incorporating into it the fictitious notion of historical antagonism.

Similarly, the respective policies of the Polish and West German governments were not conducive to lessening political differences. The recognition of the Oder-Neisse border by the German Democratic Republic in 1950 did not diminish the magnitude of the problem either, since even in the eyes of Polish Communist leadership that government lacked credibility and legitimacy. Even Bonn's tardy and cautious approach to Poland through the exchange of official Trade Missions was virtually designed to circumvent rather than resolve the cardinal problem: the unsettled question of the boundaries.

Reaction of Polish Party and Government

Neither the German Church's Memorandum nor the initiative of the Catholic bishops of Poland improved relations between the two countries. Bonn government circles maintained a conspicuously noncommittal attitude toward both messages. After two weeks of silence the Polish Communist Government and press delivered the most vicious attack since the mid-fifties on the Catholic Church of Poland.

The first criticisms were published not in official governmental Party organs like *Trybuna Ludu,* but in papers which are allegedly independent like *Zycie Warszawy.*[25] read mainly by Polish intellectuals, or even in the organ of the Catholic-oriented Pax-Movement, *Slowo Powszcechne.* Initial criticism thus came from the allegedly outraged masses, and Party and government could seem to respond to their positions rather than to have determined them. By the end of December, 1965, the official Party organ *Trybuna Ludu* and all organs of the

25. "In whose name?" *Zycie Warszawy,* December 10, 1965.

various factions of the Party, including the Catholic-oriented papers, had taken up the chorus.[26]

The Polish government accused the ecclesiastical hierarchy of having neglected the national interest and of having distorted historical facts. In doing so it made clear in the first place that the Gomulka regime did not desire a reconciliation with Germany at all. This seems to support the allegation that the perpetuation of the unsettled relationship between Poland and Germany is a substantial part of the Communist *raison d'être* in East Europe. Second, the regime's negative attitude diminished the credibility of those Western observers who have maintained that Polish Communists, with their alleged freedom to maneuver, would work to relax Cold War tensions in Europe.[27]

The Gomulka regime has since continued to block moves toward reconciliation in a number of ways. First, it has insisted that West Germany's formal recognition of existing boundaries was an indispensable prerequisite for the normalization of relations between the two countries. While this policy contains some elements of logic, it excludes the possibility of compromise between the two nations. Secondly, the Gomulka regime has identified itself with Moscow's and its German satellite's German policy to such an extent that by 1965 it could not have provided Bonn with a minimum incentive for a reconciliation, even if it had desired to do so.

Poland's increasing dependence on the Soviet Union in foreign policy could be demonstrated by its changing attitude toward the two Germanies. Poland took its last apparently independent political initiative more than twelve years ago by publishing the two Rapacki Plans which called for a nuclear-free zone in Central Europe. The Rapacki Plan of 1957 and its 1958 revision have since disappeared from the agenda of

26. "In regard to the message of the Bishops," editorial in *Trybuna Ludu*, December 12, 1965; see also the publications on December 19, 1965, of the political and cultur-political weeklies *Polityka* and *Kultura*, along with those of the *Wroclowski Tygodnik Katolicki*, as well as the corresponding articles of the nation-communist oriented faction of the Polish Partisans in *Sztander Molich* and in *Zolnierz Wolnosci* on December 18 and 20.

27. To this see the unsigned article, "Czyrankiewitz in Paris," *Die Welt*, September 18, 1966, in which the Polish President said that "The platform for a political rapprochement between Poland and Germany must be the acceptance of the status quo by the latter."

European politics. If the West had accepted either one of those Plans, the Soviet Union's offensive nuclear potential would have been strengthened enormously. A redistribution of nuclear power on the continent favorable only to the USSR was naturally unacceptable to the West.

The importance of the Rapacki Plans was that they were launched in a psychologically favorable political climate, when the new Gomulka regime, itself the result of Soviet concessions to Poland, was making serious efforts to improve its relations with the West in general and with West Germany in particular. A series of indirect preliminary discussions, such as those of Berthold Beitz, the Plenipotentiary Director General of Krupp, failed — partly because of Germany's insistence on the Hallstein Doctrine, partly on the issue of the Oder-Neisse boundary. Nevertheless there were some indications that the Gomulka regime, at least at that time, did not explicitly request formal recognition of the finality of the Oder-Neisse line as a prerequisite for normalization of Polish-German relations. It is probable that the Polish regime could have been satisfied with rather general assurances.

By 1958 Khruschev's attitude toward Bonn had hardened, and the Gomulka regime quietly shelved the Rapacki Plan. Six years later the Polish government came forward with a similar proposal, this time labeled as the Gomulka Plan. Unlike its predecessor, the Gomulka Plan was clearly inspired by the Kremlin, and was intended to supplement Khruschev's policy of coexistence. Its call for "freezing nuclear weapons" in Central Europe was designed to prevent West Germany from acquiring nuclear weapons.

The Gomulka Plan was circulated after long consultations with other East European states and the Soviets. The USSR's insistence on the "two Germanies" doctrine had by then greatly diminished the likelihood of Poland's ever facing a unified threat from across the Oder-Neisse. Practical politics dictated, therefore, that for the foreseeable future the Gomulka regime align its policy with that of the Soviet Union to its east and East Germany to its west.

Closer scrutiny of the Polish plans to bring about a European "disengagement," or to create a "demilitarized zone" in Central and Eastern Europe, or even the proposal to establish a "nuclear-free zone" in the same area strongly suggests that Polish foreign policy has in fact been designed primarily to help perpetuate Soviet predominance on the European continent. Insofar as it has aimed at the establishment of a new European security arrangement, Polish foreign policy has not sought rapprochement between Western and Eastern Europe. Nor has Poland demonstrated in its formulation of foreign policy significant independence from the Soviet Union. On the contrary, the main features of Warsaw's initiatives seem to have conformed to the unmistakable intention of the Soviet Union to seek more convenient security arrangements in Europe without creating substantial changes in the political status quo.

Two questions should be considered at this juncture. Will Bonn's recent acceptance of the Oder-Neisse boundary mean a new era in Polish-German relations? Will this step induce Poland to follow a policy more independent of Moscow? Some observers maintain that the accepting of the status quo with regard to Poland may not only serve Polish-German reconciliation, but could also initiate a new Western policy toward Eastern Europe.[28] In 1965 such recognition would certainly have eliminated one obstacle to reconciliation. One can even agree that recognition of the Oder-Neisse boundary in 1965 was a necessary precondition for eventual normalization of diplomatic relations between Poland and Germany. Such a step at that time would have reassured Poland that German leaders could at last accept the fact that a substantial change in Poland's western boundaries or a subsequent re-Germanization of Silesia or parts of Prussia was unthinkable.

Accepting the territorial status quo could not, however, in and of itself change Polish policy concerning the division of Germany since Poland also denies the validity of Bonn's claim to be the sole political representative of German interests. It is evident that both the Soviet Union and Poland have considered the division of Germany as the *other* political reality which must be accepted by Bonn. And finally, the Gomulka regime's uncompromising rejection of the ecclesiastical letter exchange

28. Zbigniew Brzezinski, *Alternative to Partition* (McGraw-Hill Book Co., New York, 1965), pp. 141 ff.

forced West German leaders and public alike to face the possibility that Bonn's Eastern policy might not produce even modest results. The need for a thoroughgoing re-examination of the Federal Republic's Eastern policy became more and more obvious.

Domestic and External Pressures

The year 1966 was a most crucial one for the Federal Republic. Bonn's foreign policy frustrations prompted the cautious abandoning of old concepts and hesitant willingness to explore new possibilities. West German leadership labored under a multitude of external and internal pressures. Concentrated diplomatic pressure from the East led by the Soviet Union was exercised to isolate West Germany diplomatically.[29] Franco-Russian rapprochement, already visible at the beginning of the year, would only increase Bonn's solitude.

France's withdrawal from NATO and her intensified diplomatic and trade relations with Eastern Europe had a profound effect on Germany. De Gaulle's policy was based on the assumption that the Soviet Union had abandoned its expansionist designs toward Western Europe. This new assessment of Soviet intentions not only brought NATO's *raison d'être* into question, it also seriously jeopardized German security. Finally, reassertion of France's diplomatic and economic presence in Eastern Europe, especially in Poland, as well as de Gaulle's repeated acceptance of the Oder-Neisse boundary, confirmed beyond doubt that France would uphold the status quo in that area.

The British and Americans also showed signs of accepting the East European status quo. The British decided to grant long-term credits to the Soviet Union and to reduce their troop strength in West Germany. American policy was far more concerned with halting nuclear proliferation and maintaining

29. *Rede des sowjetischen Aussenministers, Andrej Gromyko am 9. December 1965* (Auszug), Europa Archiv, February, 1966, pp. D88–94; see also *Neujahrsbotschaft des Staatsvorsitzenden, Walter Ulbricht, ibid.*, pp. D94–97; *Erklärung der Teilnehmerstaaten des Warschauer Vertrags vom 6. Juli 1966*, Europa Archiv, August, 1966, pp. D414–24.

military stability in Europe with the smallest possible number of troops than with solving Europe's political problems.

Demands for a fundamental rethinking of West German foreign policy were voiced inside the Federal Assembly and outside. The parliamentary opposition, the government's coalition partner and even some members of the CSU began to demand a thorough examination of West Germany's position.

An increasing number of individual voices were heard urging that alternative policies to Eastern Europe be explored. The political tastes of these individuals ranged from Freiherr von Guttenberg to the Social Democrat Herbert Wehner, or from Professor Eschenburg to Professor von Weizsaecker and even to Franz Joseph Strauss. None of these advocated accepting the Oder-Neisse border prior to a final settlement; nor did they see recognition of the GDR as the *sine qua non* of eventual German reunification. But the emerging consensus on the need for a new policy toward the East was unmistakable.

Nowhere was the growing willingness to take new initiatives more clearly in evidence than in government reaction to and news commentaries on the SED's ill-fated proposal for an open dialogue between the two Workers' Parties of two Germanies. On February 11 the East German regime's official newspaper published an Open Letter from the SED to the Social Democratic Party of Germany.[30] The Open Letter is a classic example of the East German approach to political problems. It continued appeals to the solidarity of the workers, and direct and indirect falsification of facts, including deliberate distortion of political realities. Subsequent messages from the SED were of similar caliber. The only constructive proposal embedded in all this was the SED call for a pan-German committee to explore the possibilities of "lowering or eliminating" the barriers blocking understanding between the Germanies.[31] But other than that, the SED letter called for no less than a basic and unilateral change in the principles which guided West German foreign

---

30. "Offener Brief an die Delegierten des Dortmunder Parteitages," *Neues Deutschland.* February 11, 1966; reprinted also in *Offensive Ausienander-setzung*, Pressestelle des Vorstandes der SPD, Bonn (Vorwaerts Druck, Bad Godesberg, 1966), pp. 151–62.
31. *Ibid.*, p. 161.

policy. Had the letter's tone and intent given any evidence of good faith, it might in fact have served as a point of departure for talks with the SPD, but there was no evidence of good faith to seize upon.

The SPD replied to the East German open letter on March 8.[32] The document is a testimony to Social Democratic statesmanship. The SPD identified itself firmly with the West German democratic order and unequivocally refused any overt or covert cooperation with the East German Communists, stating "... the German Social Democrats are not available for popular-front maneuvers ... for all conditions for a cooperation [between SPD and SED] are lacking."[33]

The SPD emphasized the abnormal situation created at the Berlin Wall by the Walter Ulbricht "shooting order". The reply continued, while "it is extremely difficult [for the SPD] to accept the Open Letter which bears the signature of those who could repeal the order to shoot at Germans by Germans as the basis for an open dialogue ... the Party nevertheless is willing to engage in a discussion if it is sincere and open in both parts of Germany."[34] But the West German Social Democrats made it clear that "a dialogue on the German problem ... could not be the exclusive concern of the SPD ... it is the concern of all political parties in West Germany and through them that of the German nation." Finally, the SPD stated its unswerving opposition to the communist "two-states" and declared that it was the exclusive responsibility of the East German regime to create the conditions for an acceptable modus vivendi for Germans in both halves of the divided state.

In its dealing with the East German regime the SPD must be credited with extraordinary moderation, as well as with a most realistic appraisal of the domestic limitations on its own freedom of maneuver. But the Party recognized the kernel of a constructive possibility in Pankow's message and it cautiously refrained from setting preconditions for an eventual dialogue. The hard core of the letter stressed the SPD's desire to "estab-

---

32. "Offene Antwort der SPD an die Sozialistische Einheitspartei Deutschlands," *Offensive Auseinandersetzung, op. cit.*, pp. 163–71.
33. *Ibid.*, p. 170.
34. *Ibid.*, p. 164.

lish favorable conditions for the solution of practical questions
. . . in spite of our unbridgeable differences of opinion". In a
crucial passage the SPD suggested the continuation of the
"policy of the little steps" which could make life in the divided
country more bearable, and which should strengthen the
national consciousness of all Germans. Finally, the SPD answers
suggest a "continuous dialogue" on issues like the relation of an
eventually reunited Germany with its neighbors, or the attitude
of all Germans toward an eventual general peace settlement.

As a result of subsequent exchanges of letters,[35] representatives of both parties began talks about the time and place of an
open dialogue between prominent members of the SED and
SPD. However, no sooner had a tentative agreement been
reached than the communist representatives began to procras-
tinate. After proposals and counterproposals, accusations and
distortions, the discussions ended in a stalemate.[36] Evidently
the East German leadership's original aim was to use their
Open Letter as a propaganda weapon, and it was not prepared
for the SPD's reply. When the West German Social Democrats
answered with concrete proposals, and the East German SED
had tentatively accepted the condition that their conversations
be fully covered by the mass media from both parts of Germany,
the East German communists realized they were trapped by
their own maneuver and began to back out.

The open dialogue between SPD and SED never material-
ized. But as one of the most astute foreign policy commentators
in the Federal Republic pointed out, "something happened in
Germany in 1966."[37] Indeed, one could say that the polemics
between the SPD and the East German communists was of
extraordinary importance for the subsequent development of a
consensus on Bonn's German and Eastern policies. The mere

35. "Offener Brief der SED an die Sozialdemokratische Partei Deutschlands," *Neues Deutschland*, March 25, 1966; "Zweite offene Antwort der
SPD," *Offensive Auseinandersetzung, op. cit.*, pp. 187–95; "Wortlaut der SED
Stellungnahme vom 28.4.1966," *ibid.*, pp. 196–208.
36. "Bericht der Beauftragten der SPD Fritz Stallberg und Hans Striefler
ueber die technischen Absprachen vom 5.5.1966," *Offensive Auseinandersetzung, op. cit.*, pp. 213–15.
37. Theo Sommer, "Ein Dialog zwischen Deutschen," *Die Zeit*, March 25,
1966.

fact that the two Parties from the two halves of Germany had communicated with each other for the firt time since the forced merger of the Socialist and Communist Parties in the East was seen as a positive development in West Germany. Even the ruling CDU/CSU and FDP unexpectedly gave their blessings to their parliamentary opposition. As late as 1958 Adenauer had accused Herbert Wehner, and through him the Socialist Party, of speaking the language of Pankow, and in 1959 Rainer Barzel had called the SPD's plan for Germany utopian and bordering on treason. The change of heart in the government parties by 1966 was considerable indeed.

There is reason to believe that SPD leaders hoped that their willingness to communicate with the East Germans would prod the West German government to take new initiatives itself. Both the opposition SPD and some dissident members of the government parties had urged the second Erhard government to undertake an "all encompassing inventory" of Bonn's Eastern policy. The Erhard government had promised to initiate conversations on the subject with leaders of the various parliamentary groups, then conveniently forgot the promise. Dissatisfaction with the government attitude was widespread and extended well beyond the confines of the parliament. Therefore, as one West German newspaper put it, "the SPD's thrust . . . was a hopeful symptom of encouragement for an eventual reactivation of the government's all-German policy."[38]

The SPD's cautious political reorientation, supported by the still more cautious CDU/CSU, took place in the most unfavorable political climate. Never before had it been more widely conceded that German reunification would not be achieved in the foreseeable future, and never before had the East German regime demonstrated the distressing degree of political intransigence that it did in 1966. But both government and opposition seemed to understand that eventual contacts with East Germany would be necessary to preserve a single national consciousness in the divided land. For Pankow's Open Letter campaign, far from being a sign that the idea of national solidarity was winning out over communist dogma among East German

38. "Die SPD bricht ein Tabu," *Bremer Nachrichten*, March 22, 1966.

leaders, was correctly understood as an indication that the communist regime was confident that it had at least consolidated its power.

Political Realism of thr SPD

When policy *vis-à-vis* East Germany was formulated in 1966 with the *sole* aim of preserving national solidarity in both parts of the country, the West Germans confessed much more than the fact that German national consciousness was weakening. In voluntarily limiting its political objectives in this way, Bonn in fact recognized that, though the final say would come from the Kremlin, East Germany could endorse or veto interim solutions and had to be dealt with accordingly. It would only be self-defeating to continue to pretend that "Pankow does not exist." Bonn began to accept the idea that exploratory talks, "dialogues," and eventual political contacts could serve the national interest of Germany, even if — as was the case with the verbal duel between SPD and SED — the participants spoke two different political languages. As Willy Brandt explained, "the SPD will keep the intra-German discussion alive in an offensive manner . . . because only thus could . . . [Bonn] explore what a policy without illusions could bring about."[39]

One could discern in the reactions of the West German press an unmistakable sense of relief that "after so many barren years a new beginning is in sight."[40] The SPD was credited with courage,[41] and was written of by many as a Party that had become capable of governing.[42] Some, especially at the beginning of the "dialogue,"[43] accused the SPD of engaging in a discussion of Pankow merely to quiet criticism of its foreign policy from dissident members within its own rank and file. And one must concede that the West German Social Democrats were identified with the policy platforms of the late Adenauer and subsequent Erhard regimes to such an extent

39. "An die Mitglieder der SPD," *Offensive Auseinandersetzung, op. cit.*, p. 5.
40. E. O. Maetzke, "Die Antwort der Ungefragten," *Frankfurter Allgemeine*, March 22, 1966.
41. W. H. E., "Geistige Offensive," *Die Welt*, March 21, 1966.
42. "SPD vorn," *Frankfurter Rundschau*, April 16/17, 1966.
43. "SPD und SED," *Der Tagesspiegel*, Berlin-West, March 3, 1966.

that the Party's public image suffered. The general reaction, however, was to congratulate the SPD for its cautious reassessment of political reality.

During the turbulent summer and fall of 1966, the Party's leadership continued to press in the Federal Assembly for a policy which would keep the inter-German discussion going and it also advanced a variety of semi-official propositions. Some of them were sometimes controversial, but they all bespoke the Social Democrats' determination to search for new openings in the German question.

In the fall of 1966, two SPD officials — Herbert Wehner and the Party's chief economist Schiller — advanced refreshingly unorthodox suggestions. In a television interview, Wehner suggested the establishment of an economic community between West and East Germany. In order to overcome the enormous practical problems involved in establishing an economic community between two extremely different socio-political and economic systems, Wehner suggested a gradual approach, beginning with a regulation of payments in order to ease, and later to eliminate, the "unnatural ratio between the two currencies." As the next step Wehner envisaged the establishment of a credit system, and the conclusion of long-term trade agreements, especially with regard to energy-exports (coal, electricity, etc.) to be followed by a liberal payments policy by both sides. It is evident that such close cooperation, even in embryonic form, would require the establishment of joint administrative authorities, which at a later stage could easily develop into supranational authorities similar to those of the EEC.

The suggestion to develop economic ties of this sort between the two hostile Germanies constituted an enormously important, if not entirely practicable, political initiative as well. And even though Wehner's suggestions were of questionable political value, they were definitely justified from an economic point of view. It is often forgotten that intra-German trade has technically remained trade between *two German economic regions* as it was regulated in the postwar period by the occupation authorities — a trade without customs. In this respect the Wehner proposals aimed at reviving this dormant relationship by the expansion of the volume of trade and a more rational *inter-regional* distribution of labor in the form of multifaceted economic cooperation.

The fact that both parts of Germany still enjoy a special position within the Eastern and Western blocs, moreover, means that Professor Schiller's suggestion for taking economic advantage of this would directly promote trade between East and West.

Neither the idea of establishing an economic community between two different political and economic systems, nor its political and economic implications were new. But the real significance of the Wehner and Schiller suggestions, no matter how hypothetical they may have been, was that they were an important departure from past approaches toward the intra-German problem. The willingness to sit down at the same table with representatives of an authority that formerly "did not exist," to accept the political risks inherent in an all-German common market, and to go just below the threshold of official recognition of Pankow showed great political courage. These ideas were somewhat ahead of their time, but they were a constructive answer from a responsible opposition to government impotence and public dissatisfaction with the stagnation of German policy. The socialist initiatives provided a timely outlet for widespread and growing frustration over the division in perpetuity of Germany — frustration which might otherwise have found its only focus in the re-emerging West German right.

3

the impact of
the new german right

A New German Nationalism?

It would be a difficult task to draft an objective balance sheet evaluating the impact of nationalism as a social force — now constructive, now destructive — during the 19th and 20th centuries. The fact remains that many hideous excesses have been committed in its name. The transformation of this potentially healthy ideology into fascism and National Socialism led it to be associated with intolerance, terror and destruction. It was not surprising, therefore, that the architects of the post-World War II era sought to replace nationalism with the notion of supra-nationalism. It was believed that with the help of the new ideology obsolete national boundaries would be transcended and the allegiance of the individual would be channeled from the provincial to the universal. Western Europe would be reconstructed on a far more solid political basis than before. Initial evidence that such a trend was in fact developing was impressive. The Council of Europe, the ECSC, EURATOM, and the European Economic Community testified to the practical implications of the new ideology. For a while it seemed that nationalism in Europe had finally spent its force.

Among West European states, the staunchest supporter of the

idea of European integration was the Federal Republic of Germany. Both political necessity and some political opportunism were probably interwoven with a sincere desire to be accepted by other Europeans as equals in West Europe. The Germans also had an urgent, internal need to find substitutes for lost values in the late 1940's. For all these reasons, West Germany chose "Europeanism" as its *Leitmotif*, and undertook an honest attempt to create a stable political culture in which myopic nationalism would have no place.

Nationalism was not in fact successfully eradicated: it survived in West Germany, just as it did in other European countries. There exist both the moderate nationalism of most patriotic organizations and constituent groups in the League of Expellees and the extreme nationalism found in such organizations as the Socialist Reich Party or its successor, the National Democratic Party. Whether moderate or extreme, however, nationalist groups in postwar West Germany have shown only minimal political cohesiveness. None of these organizations and small parties — except the League of Expellees, and even this only on a limited basis — have become political forces capable of influencing decisively either the formulation of foreign policy or domestic political developments. It has become commonplace to characterize West Germany's parliamentary democracy as one of the most stable political institutions of postwar Europe.

The extraordinary stability of the second German attempt at democracy can be attributed both to the absence of extreme political parties and to the two and a half party system which has resulted. This particular constellation of political forces has been ensured partly by the lack of appeal radical programs have for citizens of as post-totalitarian society living in proximity to communism, and partly by the curtailing of radical movements through judicial processes in the early 1950's. Various splinter parties disappeared from the *Bundestag* in the mid-fifties when West Germany's Electoral Laws were applied. This produced the present party system, characterized by a well-developed consensus on fundamental domestic, and, in time, on foreign policy issues. By the mid-sixties the West German party system consisted of a bourgeois-conservative

Volkspartei, the CDU/CSU; the Social Democratic Party of Germany, which successfully converted itself from a class-party to one representing the broad strata; and by the Free Democratic Party, which embraced the liberal elements of the electorate. Observers felt this system was well-nigh immutable.

In the fall of 1966, when West German consensus faced its first real test, however, a new political party emerged. In October and November, 1966, the *Nationaldemokratische Partei Deutschlands* (National Democratic Party of Germany, NPD) won eight seats in the *Landtag* of Hessen and fifteen in Bavaria. For the first time since 1953 a party of the extreme right became a factor to be reckoned with in the Federal Republic of Germany.

The fact that some 8 to 12 percent of the West German population would endorse the program of a right-wing party in local elections was profoundly shocking to some. Many jumped to unwarranted conclusions about German national character, assumed that West German democracy was in mortal danger, and even that Germany was on her way to Nazism again. While these are undeserved votes of no-confidence in West Germans and in their political system, one should nevertheless not underestimate the importance of the emergence of a political party which verges on ultra-nationalism, the vocabulary of which is unrestrained, its policies radical, and its right-wing substance undisguised.

Sigmund Neumann once contended that "political parties are the lifeline of a nation." One has to agree with Neumann that political parties generally reflect the nation's "persistent features and changing historical forms" as well as its inner dynamics and conflicts. Yet, Neumann emphasizes, political parties do not appear overnight, nor do they suddenly attract considerable segments of the electorate. If this observation is true, did the appearance of the NPD express an inner conflict of long standing? Furthermore, if there were such an inner conflict, what were its sources? Did domestic political issues play a primary role in the emergence of Germany's new right-wing extremism, or was the country's international position the primary cause? Finally, what are the prospects for continued success of a radical party in a society that has had the most disastrous experiences with extremism, and which has been exposed for more than twenty years to the successes of parliamentary democracy?

Whether under Bismarck's pseudo-parliamentarianism, or under the ill-fated democratic experience of the Weimar Republic, or under the totalitarian yoke of Hitler, German political parties have been characterized by a doctrinaire approach toward politics, a strong identification with social classes, and the absence of even a modest consensus on fundamental issues. They did not form cohesive systems of competing organizations. These very features rendered them helpless against the Nazi movement, paving the road on which German totalitarianism marched to power and in turn disrupted the development of the traditional parties.

The totality of Germany's defeat in World War II was demonstrated not only by her material exhaustion, disorganization and despair, but also by the fact that in 1945, as one German commentator remarked, German constitutional and political life had reached "point zero."[1]

Constitutional Safeguards against Extremism

Under the license and encouragement of the Allied Occupation Powers, ten parties started to represent the population. By the end of the fifties only three of these ten parties had survived in the *Bundestag*. This rather drastic numerical shift was the result, first, of the constitutional position of German political parties, and, second, of the stipulations of Bonn's Electoral Laws.

Article 21 of the Basic Law of the Federal Republic of Germany, incorporating the parties into Germany's constitutional system, grants *inter alia* the Constitutional Court the right to decide if parties "according to their aims and the behavior of their adherents seek to abolish or impair the free democratic and basic order or to jeopardize the existence of the Federal Republic of Germany."[2] The Communist Party and the

1. Walter E. Süsking, "Der politische Rohstoff," in Joachim Moras and Hans Päschke (eds.), *Deutscher Geist zwischen Gestern und Morgen* (Deutsche Verlagsanstalt, Stuttgart, 1954), p. 14.
2. *The Basic Law of the Federal Republic of Germany.*

Socialist Reich Party were barred from active participation in West German politics in 1952 and 1956, in judgments based on this Article.

The second device which greatly contributed to the parties' numerical reduction in the *Bundestag* is the Electoral Laws' provisions with regard to minor parties. In West Germany's electoral system of "personalized proportional representation"[3] a party cannot be represented in the *Bundestag* unless it receives 5 percent of the total votes cast on the Federal level or three direct mandates to be represented in the *Bundestag*. The aim of this "splinter-party" clause was to eliminate a possible source of political instability from West Germany's nascent democracy: the multiplicity of parties.

The constitutional safety-valve of Article 21, and the electoral laws undoubtedly did ensure the stability of the West German political system. This has been achieved at the cost of some sacrifice in the degree of spontaneity with which political preferences have been expressed, however. When in 1945 German political parties were permitted to re-establish themselves, within the limitations of Allied occupation policy, their development was expected to follow the French and Italian patterns. A three-party system, consisting of a Christian Democratic Right, of a Social Democratic Centre, and of a Communist Left, did seem to be evolving — but this "tripartisme" had its roots more in Allied occupation policy than in German reality. It proved to be a transient phenomenon in West Germany.

From 1947 on, as the Soviet Zone increasingly acquired the characteristics of a Russian satellite, the Western Powers began to consider the German Communist Party the agent of a dangerous adversary. At the same time, communism never regained the influence it had in the Weimar Republic after the War; it ceased to exist as a mass movement in West Germany. The resentment of millions of refugees and widespread knowledge about conditions in the Zone made the prospects for the future of the Communist Party in West Germany exceedingly

3. U. W. Kitzinger, *German Electoral Politics* (The Clarendon Press, Oxford, 1960), p. 17; see also James Pollock, "The West German Electoral Law," *The American Political Science Review*, Vol. 48, No. 2, pp. 107–31.

dim. The Party's repression in 1956 only gave belated legal sanction to widespread popular rejection of the Party.

Postwar evolution of the Right was less clear, and its ultimate elimination less successful. It is possible to say that the Right in Germany has never been able to establish a monolithic structure embracing all the rightist groups, not even under Hitler. After all, while the Nazis claimed to be the Party of the extreme Right, they also embodied "leftist" tendencies as typified by the Strasser brothers. Not only did the Hitlerian experience militate against the emergence of a unified Right in West Germany, but also when the Socialist Reich Party (SRP) was established, it did not have a convincing program. Its clearly discernible neo-nazistic tendencies, totalitarian, antiparliamentarian and racist ideology, and leadership consisting of former Nazis were repulsive even to the right-oriented electorate. The party was banned in 1952.[4]

The German Right followed two different courses. Some joined either the German Reich Party (*Deutsche Reichspartei*), a somewhat less radical edition of the SRP, or the *Bayern Partei*, which was local and conservative. Others became active within the three political parties which still functioned on the national level. The conservative element, typified by former Transport Minister Seebohm, tended to concentrate in the small *Deutsche Partei*, which survived in the *Bundestag* as long as it maintained a working arrangement with the CDU. Liberal minded nationalists joined the Free Democratic Party (FDP), the third to survive in the *Bundestag*. The rest entered the ranks of the CDU. Dispersed among the splinter parties which soon lost national importance and absorbed — partly into the national-liberal party and partly into the governing party — the Right was unable to develop even a German "Gaullisme." The result of this process was that the Right saturated the middle political sector, a development not foreseen either by the Allied Powers or by the Germans themselves.

This caused a major shift in West Germany's political equilibrium. The Social Democratic Party, originally designed by the Allied Powers as a party of the Middle, evolved into a

---

4. Cf. Alfred Grosser, *Die Bonner Demokratie* (Karl Rauch Verlag, Düsseldorf, 1960), pp. 120 ff.

party of the Left. The CDU/CSU, intended as an expression of bourgeois-conservative trends on the other hand, emerged as the party of the centre. Finally, the Right, heterogeneous as it was, functioned not as an independent unit, but as a conglomeration of "anti-Marxist," conservative and moderately nationalist groups. This shift produced Bonn's three-party system with what most observers felt were all the necessary conditions for political stability, with the qualification that the real right and left were missing.

To expect that legally banning organized extremism would also silence the extremists themselves was political naivety. Barring a party from the political scene is not equivalent to the elimination of rightist, ultra-conservative and nationalistic sentiment. Such sentiment did indeed survive in postwar Germany. From the first days of the Federal Republic a series of radical, rightist groups have represented a small but important segment of the electorate. The parties that sought the support of these right, radical Germans were numerous, but their basic tenets were fervently nationalist, frequently bordering on the extremes. Most of these parties were reduced to political unimportance even at the local level, or disappeared completely. But their scattered followers remained, and the three great parties succeeded in attracting only a part of them. The rest voted for a new party in the fall of 1966.

The Profile of a New Extreme Right

The National Democrat Party (NPD) was founded in 1964, and its membership had risen from a modest 6,000 to about 31,000 by 1967. What is this new Party? What is the social stratification of its membership? What are the ages and the educational levels of those who have endorsed the party's program? Finally, what is the program of the party that has succeeded in attracting a considerable segment of the electorate in six of the ten Federal States?

Although the data in Table I are by no means complete, the information available in 1967 permitted some tentative conclusions. They clearly show that the NPD does not follow the traditional pattern of German political parties insofar as it cannot be identified with any one social class. In this the NPD has much in common with the three "establishment" parties, all of which cut across all social strata. Aside from this fact, several other observations could be made. First, no other German political party has a membership which is as much as 71 per cent male. This unusual proportion may indicate that the membership is rather active. The second important observation is the fact that the membership's educational level is comparatively high. Sixty-eight percent has finished primary school, 11 percent high school, and 21 percent has been educated at the university level. The data imply not only that the membership demonstrates a keen interest in politics, but also that it is intellectually equipped to evaluate and interpret events of political importance. The majority of the party's supporters is recruited from the middle class. It should be pointed out, however, that this middle-class majority is very slight: 54 percent, composed of members of the upper-middle class and white-collar groups, as against the 46 percent of workers and small peasants.

The party's appeal within various age groups is also instructive. That the age group 16–29 represents only 23.7 per cent of the total membership should be encouraging, for it indicates the lack of appeal of extremism on the postwar generation. This finding is seemingly contradicted by the fact that at major universities student groups have attempted to organize themselves into NPD-oriented associations. However, not even the establishment of the Association of National Democratic University Students (*Nationaldemokratische Hochschulgruppen*) in Tübingen, Bonn, Mainz, Frankfurt, and Heidelberg, etc., should give cause for alarm. Although the leadership of these groups claims that they represent about 7 to 9 percent of these student bodies and includes some faculty as well, in fact their followers number only 30–40 students out of 11,000 in Tübingen, or at other universities.[5] Moreover, the NPD-oriented university groups have encountered vigorous opposition from other non-rightist groups.

The bulk of the NPD's membership is composed of the age

5. "NPD-Hochschulgruppen: Heil Hitler," *Der Spiegel*, January 23, 1967, p. 37.

TABLE I[6]

BY SEX:	Percentage
Male	71
Female	29
BY AGE:	
16–29	23.7
30–44	27.6
45–64	37.6
65 and over	11.1
BY DENOMINATION:	
Protestant	63
Catholic	28
Other	9
BY OCCUPATION:	
Academicians, highranking civil servants and officers, students	6
Self-employed	25
Civil service and professional army	7
Clerical workers	18
Workers	27
Housewives	6
Pensioners	11

group between 30 and 60 years, i.e. those born between 1907 and 1936–7 constitute a 61 percent majority of the Party. In this group those between 30 and 44 years are represented by 30 percent, those between 45 and 60 by 31 percent. These age groups form 50 percent of the total population of the Federal Republic. The age group over 60 forms only 16 percent of the party, in contrast to 23 percent of the total population of West Germany. The core of the NPD is therefore made up by those generations which were exposed not only to the ill-fated

6. The data for this table and for the associated text have been compiled from the findings of the following sources: "Rechts-radikalismus in der Bundesrepublik im Jahre 1966," *Aus Politik und Zeitgeschichte*, June 14, 1967 (Bundeszentrale für politische Bildung, Bonn, 1967), pp. 3–38. The pamphlet is a reprint of the report of the *Bundesministerium des Innern* and should be considered as authentic. See also: E. P. Neumann, "Steckbrief einer radikalen Partei," *Die Zeit*, January 24, 1967: "NPD-Erfolg unter der Lupe," *Neue Zürcher Zeitung*, November 22, 1966, p. 5.

TABLE I (cont.)

BY CLASS:	Percentage
Upper middle class	28
Lower middle class	26
Manual workers	38
Lowest social strata	8
BY EDUCATION:	
Junior high	68
High school and college	32
BY POPULATION DISTRIBUTION:	
Villages (under 2,000)	23
Towns (2,000–20,000)	24
Medium cities (20,000–100,000)	18
Large cities (over 100,000)	35
BY NATIONALITY:	
Indigenous	73
Expellees and refugees	27

democratic experience of the Weimar Republic but also to the indoctrinative influences of the Third Reich.

The strongest single social group is the middle class, with 50 percent. If one includes the housewives and pensioners in this category, the proportion is even greater: 67 percent. The next largest social group is the workers, with 27 percent. Thus, the backbone of the Party seems to be middle-class and "petit bourgeois" (blue and white collar) elements. Since none of these strata, including the industrial workers, could be considered as the stepchildren of the "Wirtschaftswunder," the notion that the preference for radicalism has been nurtured by social position can be discarded. The overwhelmingly middle-class composition of the party is reflected in part by the fact that the membership is recruited mostly from small towns (24 percent), and from middle-sized cities (18 percent).

The proportion between refugees from the Eastern territories and the local population is 27 to 73 percent. This is close to the composition of the population of West Germany at large: 24 percent refugees and 76 percent indigenous West Germans.

Most indicative of the Party's true character is the political background of its membership. According to the Ministry of the Interior report, approximately 2,000 of the Party's present members had joined the NSDAP before the 1933 "Machtergreifung." The percentage of "old-timers" (Alt-Parteigenossen) within the NPD is eight times their proportion in the overall population of the Federal Republic. In addition to the pre-1933 members of the Nazis we also find within the ranks of the NPD hundreds of former Nazi functionaries who joined the Hitler movement after 1933. The second largest contingent in the NPD are those who one time or another either belonged to the rightist-radical organizations during the early years of the Federal Republic or were members of the Socialist Reich Party which was outlawed in 1952. Some 3,500 of the NPD's present members were formerly members of the German Reich Party, and approximately 4,000–5,000 belonged to one or another of those rightist-radical organizations which, though never prohibited, have disappeared from the political scene. Altogether, former Nazis, people with radical leanings, and former members of extremely radical and nationalist groups constitute some 35 percent of the total membership of the National Democratic Party of Germany.

This rather high percentage is clearly represented in the Party's leadership at all levels of its organization. Although the Party claims that it is definitely not under the political and ideological influence of radical rightist elements, this contention has been contradicted by official statistical facts. More than 45 percent of the party functionaries at the community level are either former members of right radical organizations, or are Nazi "old-timers." At the county and district levels this already high proportion is 61 percent, and at the *Land* and Federal level it climbs to 67 percent. But those with a history of radical right affiliation reach their highest proportion within the Party's executive committee, and among the "official speakers for the Party" ("Bundesrednern") at 76 percent.

This brief survey of statistical data indicates that a predominantly middle-aged group of rather heterogeneous social composition has been attracted by this radical political movement. A majority of the members are from the middle class and its program reflects something of the position, grievances and expectations of the middle clss in a modern industrial world.

The Party's Appeal to a Broad Social Strata

Although its program[7] contains traces of Nazi ideology, the NPD does not seem to be fundamentally neo-fascist.[8] The program does emphasize the importance of the middle class, allegedly threatened by the powerful upper classes and by the organized working class, and it is true that the same sentiments were expressed by Nazi ideology. Demands for the development of a "sense of community instead of group interests"[9] are similarly reminiscent of some postulates of the National Socialists, who stated that the general welfare is more important than that of the individual. In advocating a change in the relationship between workers and owners, saying that in factories, where the owner is the "leader" and the workers are the "followers," the "working peace should be based on a firm relationship of trust,"[10] the party demonstrates antiunion tendencies, as well as a desire to return to pre-industrial patriarchal structures. This anti-union agitation, and the injection of the "leadership principle" ("Führerprinzip") into the economy also had its equivalent in fascist ideology.

However, the electoral successes of the NPD cannot be attributed to a program which is confused, and is certainly incomprehensible to the average voter. The NPD's emergence as a new political force in West Germany is the result of the interaction of a variety of factors: first, the campaign tactics involving skillful manipulation of truths, half-truths and outright falsifications; second, the party's calculated appeal to growing nationalist sentiment in West Germany; third, the domestic

7. *Manifest der Nationaldemokratischen Partei Deutschlands* (Vorstand der Nationaldemokratischen Partei Deutschlands, Hamburg, 1965).
8. As arguments to this point see: Dietrich Strothmann, "Der Aufmarsch der Spiesser," *Die Zeit*, November 15, 1966, and R. Kuehnl, "Neofascism on the Rise," *Review of International Affairs*, Belgrade, February 20, 1967, pp. 11–13, and *ibid.*, March 5, 1967, pp. 8–11.
9. Grundsätze . . . , *op. cit.*, Art. 1.
10. *Ibid.*, Art. III; see also: "Anmerkungen zum Manifest und zu den Grundsätzen der NPD," published by *Deutsche Nachrichten*, Hanover, January, 1967.

political crisis of the fall of 1966; and last but not least, the rapidly changing relationship between Bonn and its Western allies, which raised questions of security, reunification, and, beyond these, the future of Germany.

The NPD's successes at the polls in four of the Länder demonstrate its successful appeal to almost all social strata. The party has described itself as a *Volkspartei*. It has shown itself friendly toward workers, and has simultaneously courted the peasantry. As early as 1967 the president of the Organization of German Peasants (*Deutscher Bauernverband*), Edmund Rehwinkel, assumed that in the future some one hundred thousand peasants would vote for the NPD.[11] The reason for this sympathy from a usually conservative group is the peasantry's discontent with the government's subvention policy, which in turn is blamed on unnecessary and unsuccessful sacrifices made by Germany to the EEC. The party also purports to be the defender of the middle class, and especially of the small German entrepreneur, in vigorously opposing the "suffocating presence" of foreign firms and capital in Germany: a related theme in its thundering against the excesses of monopoly capitalism.

Particular attention has been lavished on the German soldier.[12] The NPD demands that the *Bundeswehr* (Federal Army) be placed under a German supreme command, and promises the German soldier an upgrading of his position in the society. On one hand, the party skillfully exploited the leadership crisis in the armed forces just before the 1966 elections, which had raised the question of the Federal Army's *raison d'être*. On the other hand, the party has been trying to appeal to officers who deplore the absence of military and historical traditions in the army.

Subjects which have lent themselves to easy exploitation by the German right have included the complex psychological impact of the "20th July" observations of the anniversary of Nazi military defeat and the fact that the officer corps no longer enjoys the status of a privileged class within German society.

11. "Ein Paar hunderttausend Bauern wählen NPD," *Der Spiegel*, February 13, 1967, pp. 27–35.
12. "Der Dienst ist mir absolut zu schlapp," *Der Spiegel*, February 2, 1967, pp. 26–28.

Questions such as the collective responsibility of the German General Staff prior to and during the War and the execution of high ranking officers of the former *Wehrmacht* as war criminals have also been used as propaganda levers during the election campaigns. Moreover, the party has incessantly pushed for a greater and stronger army, the spirit of which should be rooted in German tradition. In maintaining that "as long as their fathers can be publicly branded as war criminals, our men cannot be good soldiers of the fatherland," the party presents itself as a champion of a rather vocal popular sentiment which demands the termination of war crimes trials and the proclamation of a general amnesty. Finally, the tendentious nature of the appeal to the national consciousness of the German soldier is unmistakable in such election slogans as "the German soldier can no longer remain the mercenary of alien interests."[13] Although a few officers now serving in the Federal Army have been elected to the local Parliaments, and although the followers of the NPD in the armed forces are estimated by some to be as high as 25 percent, other findings suggest that a more realistic estimate is probably between 10 and 15 percent.[14] Whichever figure one accepts, the fact remains that a right radical party has made significant incursions within the Federal Army.

Foreign Policy: Old Wine in a New Bottle

The vocabulary of the NPD has been vulgar and its polemical style highly demagogic: both remind one of the ultra-rightist-nationalistic slogans of the 1920's. During the election campaigns the "establishment" parties were accused of mismanagement of the state. The Federal Republic's financial contributions to the maintenance of NATO forces in Germany were called tribute payments. West Germany's association with the Western powers was denounced as a "policy of fulfillment," a clear and malicious reference to Streseman's foreign policy in

13. *Ibid.*, p. 27; see also: "Deutscher Nationalismus — Marke NPD," *Neue Zürcher Zeitung*, November 25, 1966, III, p. 2.
14. "Der Dienst . . . ," *op. cit.*, p. 28; cf. *Institut für Demoskopie*, Allensbach, January, 1967. As to the question of the Party's attitude toward the problem of collective guilt, see Winston S. Churchill, "Mein Grossvater ist für sie ein Kriegsverbrecher," *Der Spiegel*, January 9, 1967, p. 37.

the twenties. Unfavorable comparisons were made between some aspects of present foreign policy and the foreign policy of the Weimar Republic; the presence of foreign troops in West Germany has struck a particularly sensitive nerve.[15]

The party has been deliberately ambiguous with regard to the question of Germany's borders. It has proclaimed rather equivocally that Germany has valid title to those territories "in which the German nation existed for several hundred years" — an expandable formula that might include a Germany between the Maas and Memel, and from the Rhine to the easternmost boundaries of Prussia.[16]

In order to establish German sovereignty over the lost territories, the NPD has developed a disingenuous and fantasy-ridden foreign policy posture that it calls "Realpolitik," or "practical politics". It describes itself as the "political movement for a united Germany within a united Europe." The new Europe is seen as a Confederation of the Fatherlands, presumably on the de Gaulle model, a new power center maneuvering between East and West. The NPD insists that such a Europe, economically and technically superior to the East, could and should exert pressure on the Soviet Union for the reunification of Germany. As late as 1966, the NPD further declared that the new Europe, led by France and Germany, should side temporarily with Communist China, thus applying sufficient political pressure on the Soviet Union to force it to revive its policy *vis à vis* the former German territories East of the Elbe. The reasoning behind such assertions seems particularly unsound when one takes into account the fact that in the NPD's vocabulary, "former German territories" include much more than Pomerania, Silesia and East Prussia. In the NPD's own words, "For us there are no such things as Kaliningrad, Wroclaw, Gdansk or Cheb — we recognize only Königsberg, Danzig, Breslau and Eger."

The dominant domestic political issues during the election

15. Werner Höfer, "Sie wollen den Bonnern Beine machen," *Die Zeit*, November 15, 1966, p. 3; see also: "The Collapse of an Illusion," *Frankfurter Rundschau*, November 8, 1966; reprinted in *The German Tribune*, November 19, 1966, p. 3.
16. Manifest, *op. cit.*, Art. IX.

campaigns of 1966 on the *Landtage* level were governmental crisis and the scepter of economic depression. The policies of the political parties represented in the Federal Assembly were distorted. It was alleged that the "establishment" parties did not represent the real political and economic interests of the electorate. After the two main parties joined in the Grand Coalition, it was claimed more and more insistently that the population had been denied any choice among political alternatives.

The German population's apprehension about a possible depression was ruthlessly exploited by the NPD. The dismissal of a few hundred workers in some branches of heavy industry was represented as an unmistakable sign of creeping unemployment. In August, 1966, when the coal industry closed down a few inefficient mines in the Ruhr, the NPD stridently advised that "The silent mines in the Ruhr should serve as a warning to the other branches of German industry that have been flooded and dominated by foreign capital."

Finally, the NPD has made a concerted effort to characterize itself as a "party of victory." Its speakers boisterously referred to the Party's increased victories at the polls since its establishment, beginning with the municipal elections in Schleswig, Bavaria, and Hamburg in March, 1966, through the rather spectacular by-elections in Hamelin, in September, to the *Landtag* elections in Bavaria and Hesse. While the NPD did actually increase the votes cast for it in all these elections, the total number of voters had also doubled or tripled over those who turned out in the Federal Assembly a few months earlier. Placed in proper perspective, then, NPD boasts of 200 and 300 percent gains seem deceptive at best.

The appeal to almost all social strata, the attempt to infiltrate the armed forces, the accusations of political mismanagement by established parties, and the demagogic rhetoric of the party inescapably remind one of Nazi methods. Yet the party's top leadership, none of them seriously incriminated by their behavior in the Third Reich, has not for a moment ceased to pay tribute to the constitution. How much of this devotion to constitutional order stems from the leadership's fear of possible prohibition of the party is difficult to ascertain. This considera-

tion, as well as an admixture of sincerity,[17] have in all probability both prompted the NPD's second and third rank of
leadership to pay more than lip service to the Basic Law of the
Federal Republic. The party has likewise been very careful not
to place formerly incriminated Nazis in the first lines of its
leadership in order to disarm its severest critics. Finally, the
National Democrats have been anxious to create the image of a
party which seeks "to establish the unity of Germany within
the framework of a united and independent Europe,"[18]
through strictly legal and democratic means. It is thus difficult
to accuse the NPD of being openly hostile toward the state.

Verbal and written assurances by NPD leaders notwithstanding, proponents and critics alike have readily understood
that the Party's appeal is to the virulent nationalism of an
earlier Germany. In speeches and publications the Party advo-
cates the return to "pure Germanism." The mass media has
been a primary target, for, according to NPD propaganda, it
bears primary responsibility for alleged degermanization and
demoralization of West German society. The Party is uncompromising toward the purported monopoly of an unscrupulous
clique which is said to have planned the undermining of German national, ethical and moral values. The rise of juvenile
delinquency, the "degradation of the German women," and
the complete loss of "national self-respect" in Germany are
identified as results of this process.[19] The cure prescribed for
"these foreign inspired diseases" is, predictably, a return to the
old German national values. So far the Party has stopped short
of identifying exactly what these values are.

Advocacy of "return to national consciousness" on the
domestic scene has been coupled with anti-Americanism, and
with a melodramatic and distorted view of Germany's allegedly
inferior position in the world. Washington-Bonn relations
were said to be those between overlords and vassals. Declarations that "Germany's freedom of action is limited by the
Pentagon" or "the Federal Republic is, under the prevailing

17. W. S. Churchill, *op. cit.*, p. 27.
18. Grudsätze . . . , *op. cit.*, Art. VIII.
19. James Cameron, "A Shadow no Longer than a Crooked Cross," *The
New York Times Magazine*, September 11, 1966, pp. 94–99.

conditions, an American colony" were frequent in campaign speeches. The stationing of NATO troops in the Federal Republic has also been attacked. The NPD describes them as "occupation Armies" on the one hand, and identifies lack of self-respect the reason for their continued presence on the other. Stationing foreign troops in Germany is said to be part and parcel of the West's policy of keeping "the myth of the German guilt alive." The myth of German guilt in turn enables the enemies of the nation to "extort Germany for an unlimited period of time."

This inchoate collection of demagogical phrases, undigested foreign policy concepts, half-truths and deliberate distortions has been laced through with a sentimental appeal to the German population's consciousness of "The People (Volk), Fatherland and History." When the NPD says that "Only a nation, conscious of its own worth, and of its national honor, can earn the respect and friendship of other nations," it implies that German dignity and honor were destroyed by foreign conquerors in 1945, and that the same powers and those who did their bidding had subsequently suppressed the most precious attributes of German national character.

While one should not overestimate the importance of the phenomenon, the Party's electoral successes in 1966 have demonstrated a disturbing conceptual confusion in certain segments of the West German electorate. The NPD's evocative phrases about "national consciousness," "national dignity and honor," and "exploitation by foreign powers," and its pointed comments about the supposed intellectual laziness and political immaturity of the masses, have released explosive emotions in Germany — emotions which in 1966 may have been politically no less dangerous than they were in the Weimar Republic, even though they were shared by a smaller percentage of the population.

But alarming as the NPD's successes may have appeared in 1966–7, its room for political maneuver was limited and its prospects for entering the *Bundestag* in 1969 were not promising. Party leaders had publicly hoped for 8 to 12 percent of the vote in the 1969 Federal elections,[20] but when the returns came in it

20. "Im Bundestag wird alles anders aussehen" (Spiegel-Gespräch mit dem

was apparent that — with a scant 4.3 percent of the total —
the NPD had not even captured the minimum 5 percent which
would allow it a place in the Federal Assembly. Nor has the
Party enjoyed significant new successes since 1969. The June,
1970, by-elections in Lower Saxony, Saar, and Bavaria eliminated the NPD as a serious political factor even on the local
level. In none of these three states did the Party get more than
3.3 percent of the votes cast, and it was even defeated in
Hanover, the home district of its top leader. Finally, in November, 1970, the Party was also eliminated from Hesse, again
receiving only 3.3 percent of the votes cast. From the vantage
point of the present day, the NPD no longer seems to threaten
to be a catalyst of a revived German nationalism.

Such a sudden decline in the fortunes of the NPD could not
have been foreseen in 1967 or 1968, however, and the rise of
the NPD in the mid-sixties still requires some careful explanation. It would be circular reasoning to attribute the emergence
of the NPD as a political factor in the Federal Republic to a
sudden outburst of latent nationalism and too facile to explain
it away in terms of the questionable organizational talents of
the Party's leadership. The causes of the rise of a new radical
Right in Germany must be sought elsewhere: namely, in the
domestic political consequences of Bonn's changing relationship with the West, a new state of affairs for which West
German society seems to have been politically and morally unprepared.

The Dilemma of Nationalism vs. Supra-nationalism

Wilhelm Grewe, then Ambassador of the Federal Republic
in Washington, concluded his classic study of postwar German
foreign policy in 1960 with the unanswered question whether
or not "the Western World possesses sufficient moral strength
to reject the temptations of comforting illusions, and to accept
the sacrifices, self-denials and strains"[21] which will be demanded
of it by the coming decade. In the same year, another author
expressed some anxiety regarding the possible impact of

NPD-Vorsitzenden Adolf von Thadden), *Der Spiegel*, Vol. 23, No. 22 (May
26, 1969), pp. 36–39.
21. Grewe, *op. cit.*, p. 448.

Chancellor Adenauer's patriarchal rule on the future of Bonn's democracy, saying:

> The mechanism of democracy will, perhaps, function smoothly once Adenauer leaves the [political] scene. It is to be feared, however, that the people will judge too harshly the rivalries, uncertainties, and changes which are certain to ensue, unaware of the fact that these are the unavoidable disadvantages of democracy.[22]

Both these authors were writing at the end of the first decade of West Germany's existence, during which there had been nothing less than a gargantuan attempt at complete and fundamental reorientation of German domestic and foreign policies. This effort, had, firstly, resulted in the inclusion of Germany into a cohesive Western World. Second, it induced the Germans to weigh their position in the world from a less narrowminded national point of view. Last but not least, the process of reorientation tied Germany firmly to a group of states with which it developed a community of interest. Even from outside the Federal Republic one could discern the unmistakable end of Germany's longstanding isolation in the international community, and the beginning of the habit of understanding the German problem in the larger framework of broader European and Atlantic affairs.

West Germany's Western-oriented policy during its first ten years was undeniably determined in the first instance by the exigencies of its status as successor state to a defeated power. For since the new state was established upon the initiative and with the encouragement of the West as a bulwark against communism in the East, an exclusive Western orientation was virtually a necessary condition for survival itself during its first years. Germany, divided and still burdened with the consequences of its failures as a nation-state, could hardly use the discredited national idea as the cornerstone of its new political edifice. The postwar concept of "Europe" provided the Germans with an escape from historical isolation, and from the material and spiritual miseries of the status of defeated power.

The German people and their new leaders embraced the

22. Alfred Grosser, *op. cit.*, p. 421.

new Europeanism — and did so on the whole spontaneously and sincerely. The Germans, and for that matter other Europeans as well, hoped that in doing so they would accomplish much more than merely overcoming their national-socialist past. A united Europe was seen as a framework which could supercede the bankrupt 19th-century idea of the sovereign nation-state, which had led to so much tragedy in the past, and Europeanism seemed at once more appealing and more practical than the nation-state and its corollary, nationalism, had ever been.

It may well be that the heady notion of supra-nationalism was stressed by many European statesmen at the expense of sober scrutiny of the historical and political givens from which it had to be constructed. It is true that there were unmistakable elements of utopian thinking in the optimism of the would-be architects of the new Europe. But the West Germans were perhaps more aware than most of some of the shortcomings of the new idea — by making their foreign policy a decidedly European one — they did bridge the intellectual and ideological gap which had separated them for so long from the rest of Europe.

The question which the events of the mid-fifties force one to consider is: did Germany's Western orientation create a solid, permanent and shock-resistant political basis for the future? For one thing, the nature of Germany's orientation toward the West left its leaders with few guidelines to follow in the event of the disintegration of the Alliance. West Germans were quite unprepared to choose among the competing varieties of Western policy which in the sixties replaced the formerly more or less homogeneous Western posture.

Furthermore, there had been basic agreement between the rest of the West and Bonn that the former would continue to regard the latter as the sole spokesman for all Germans in general, and that in particular the West would not prevent the re-establishment of a unitary German state. The year between the second Berlin crisis and the erection of the Berlin Wall were those in which Bonn's original understanding with the West was seriously eroded. Following Khrushchev's 1958 ultimatum demanding a radical change in Berlin's status, West Germany was plunged into pessimism and gloom. West Germany's lack of confidence was deepened by the painfully obvious vacillation of her allies. While neither the status of Berlin was altered, nor the existence of the Federal Republic seriously endangered in or after 1958, the possibility that a compromise solution over Berlin at Bonn's expense might eventually be sought was raised. Finally, the West's tacit acceptance of a divided Germany greatly contributed to further disillusionment and frustration in Bonn. But when in the mid-sixties it became necessary to ask what would happen if this understanding were not honored by one of the contracting parties, neither West Germany policy makers nor the public had firm answers.

The Western Alliance's change of heart left West Germans in a sort of lonely confusion — a state of mind that was fertile soil for a negative reaction beyond the control of either government or loyal opposition. Indeed, the failure of either government or parliamentary opposition to produce constructive proposals for a new foreign policy which could deal effectively with the changed international situation understandably weakened the confidence of the electorate.

While the emergence of the new German Right can be explained in part by the real or imagined failures of the West in its European or German policy, another and equally important contributing factor has been de Gaulle. It was de Gaulle who blocked the evolution of the kind of Europe upon which Bonn's foreign policy had been predicated. And, predictably, de Gaulle's reinvigoration of the concept of the nation-state created serious dilemmas for Germans: the integrity of the nation-state is neither a political reality for them, nor could it be achieved by following the Gaullist blueprint. The anomalous version of Gaullism that did take root in West Germany was unaware of its own contradictory nature. Those who embraced de Gaulle's policies in Germany failed to understand that, of all the states of West Europe, the Federal Republic could least afford to adopt a policy which envisages a Europe without a strong American presence. To do so would be to undermine one of the necessary preconditions of West Germany's security as a state.

In 1964, amid symptoms of growing malaise in the population, the NPD was established. The feeling of deep-seated disappointment and widespread frustration grew during 1965 and 1966, as West German foreign policy continued devoid of serious initiatives, demonstrating the helplessness and confusion of government leaders. Bonn's ties with the West resembled a Gordian knot which became increasingly difficult to disentangle. The resulting sense of insecurity precipitated the worst domestic political crisis of the Federal Republic's short history.

Domestic Crisis and the Great Coalition

The 1966 crisis over the impasse in Bonn's foreign policy was intensified by adverse developments in the manner in which politics was conducted domestically: normal political discussion degenerated into uncontrollable quarreling, and the democratic process was itself discredited in the eyes of an increasingly skeptical electorate that could not help recalling the undignified agonies of Weimar democracy. Evidence of incompetence within the governing party grew along with signs that it sought more and more to bypass the democratic process and make dangerously independent policy decisions. Because it was primarily the governing party which was stigmatized by evidence of political decay while the opposition's image remained relatively untarnished, Bonn was in fact left with a democratic alternative.

However, Bonn's domestic political crisis unfolded in the shadow of its foreign policy crisis, a policy to which there has been no obvious, rational alternative for the Federal Republic. This difficult situation was masterfully exploited by the NPD. The opportunities for its electoral successes were provided by the Bonn government. Only under circumstances of enormous distress and official confusion could the National Democratic Party have presented itself as an acceptable alternative to the electorate with even the slim chances for success it in fact had.

The events of 1966 demonstrated that, twenty-one years after the catastrophic end of the frenzied nationalism of the Third Reich, it was again possible to mobilize a considerable segment of the German electorate by manipulating their national emotions. It would be false with regard to 1966 — or today — to over-dramatize this new upsurge of national sentiment. It has no political future in the Federal Republic, despite some similarities with events of the summer and fall of 1929, when the Nazis, spurred by the pending economic depression, intensified political agitation, and made headway in local electtions.

Fortunately, the appeal of the NPD was evaluated correctly by most Germans in 1966, and its electoral successes were seen at the time in their proper proportions. Confusion of the sort that hastened the fall of the Weimar Republic did not occur. NPD successes did not seriously weaken the structure of either one of the great political parties. Eight, ten or even twelve percent of the total votes cast in favor of a radical nationalistic Party might have spread alarm in Germany of the sixties, except that against these numbers stood the solid 88 percent of the voters who endorsed one or the other of the established parties. In Bonn it was understood that the further development of the NPD depended on the leading political groups' reaction to this discomforting new presence on the political scene as well as to the conditions which had favored its sudden growth.

By November both government and opposition saw the need for a thoroughgoing reappraisal of West German foreign policy. Only by formulating a practical alternative to the frustrating *immobilisme* of the early sixties, could the leading Parties nip the new nationalistic trend in the bud. This would entail a searching revision of the fundamental tenets of Bonn's foreign policy in the entire postwar period. The first step would have to be accepting Europe's mood of *détente*, and the formulation of a fundamentally new policy toward Eastern Europe in general and East Germany in particular.

Such a major about-face was to be accomplished only by installing new leadership within the governing CDU and by altering in the whole composition of the government itself. There were many long weeks of political horse-trading. All parties involved presented the electorate with a dispiriting view of some of the ugliest aspects of the democratic process. Finally, however, the Great Coalition, composed of Christian Democratic Union and Social Democrats, was established. On December 13, the new Federal Chancellor presented his governmental program to the Federal Assembly, the foreign policy parts of which were most favorably received. The new Kiesinger-Brandt foreign policy, which entailed a radically changed approach toward Eastern Europe in general and East Germany in particular, deserves a detailed analysis.

4

a
new eastern policy

Pragmatism, "Détente" and Reconciliation

Kurt Georg Kiesinger, the new Federal Chancellor, presented the coalition government's program to the Federal Assembly on December 13, 1966. The foreign policy sections clearly reflected the spirit of *détente* which permeated the West during and after 1966: never had a West German government's official statement of its foreign policy position been characterized by such moderation and straightforward sobriety. It was clear that the difficult negotiations that created the Grand Coalition of West Germany's two major parties had also involved a creative and long-overdue re-evaluation of the country's changing international position.

The coalition government's foreign policy guidelines bore the unmistakable stamp of the Social Democratic half of the partnership. The SPD had been on record since 1959 in favor of just such a cautious but practical opening toward the East as that anticipated by the coalition program. The document's tone was also much influenced by the new Chancellor himself. His devotion to Europeanism, his congenital sympathy toward France as a nation, and his political personality — that of the great coordinator — were woven through the text. The third major ingredient in the document was the new coalition's obvious desire to respond to urging from Washington and Paris for active West German participation in the relaxation of international tension which, it was widely hoped, might lead eventually to a new and more acceptable security arrangement for the continent.

There are two striking features of the Grand Coalition's December declaration: first, absolute willingness to approach East Europe in a conciliatory spirit in hopes of a thorough normalization of relations; and, concomitantly, Bonn's clear determination that any such new approaches to Communist East Europe be pursued within the general framework of the search for *détente* by the Federal Republic's allies in the West.[1] This stance was designed to reverse West Germany's perilous drift toward political isolation within the Western camp on the one hand, and to infuse new vitality into its position toward Eastern Europe on the other.

The list of political offerings from the Great Coalition to the Kremlin was, perforce, limited by the Soviet Union's unwillingness to so much as enter into diplomatic conversations on the German question. It contained a renewed proposal for mutual renunciation of the use of force in settling political problems, and declared Bonn's intention to seek "intensified understanding and trust . . . through the development of economic and cultural relations."[2] The hope was expressed that the Soviet Union, convinced by the sincerity of the new West German government to work toward a genuine relaxation of tensions, would at long last consent to a reopening of the German question.[3] In light of the multitude of unsolved political problems between Bonn and Moscow, the above list may seem scant. Yet the plea for a mutual renunciation of the use of force and the expressed hope for a conciliatory attitude on the part of the Soviets did accurately communicate the Coalition's fundamental goal: to create an international climate which would favor further initiatives toward *détente*.

1. "Regierungserklärung von Bundeskanzler Dr. Kurt Georg Kiesinger vor dem Deutschen Bundestag am 13. Dezember 1966," *Bulletin des Presse- und Informationsamtes der Bundesregierung* (hereafter *Bulletin*), No. 157, 14. Dezember, 1966; also reprinted in excerpts in *Europa Archiv*, Vol. 22, No. 1, pp. D15–19.   2. *Ibid.*, p. D16.   3. *Loc. cit.*

The new Kiesinger government used a more conciliatory tone toward East Europe than it did toward the Soviet Union. The statement that the new government would continue to regard Germany as a bridge between East and West, and in the assurance that "we would like to act according to the demands of . . . such a position"[4] was not new. Nor was the expressed desire to improve all aspects between West Germany and her Eastern neighbors strikingly new. But Chancellor Kiesinger's declaration that Bonn was ready to "improve all aspects of political relations [with our Eastern neighbors] wherever this is permitted by . . . [political] circumstances"[5] was of utmost importance. The reference to "political circumstances" implied that Bonn would be willing to improve these circumstances by abandoning or modifying its own approach toward Eastern Europe if necessary.

In keeping with its sober and open tone, the coalition program also defined the limits beyond which the Great Coalition was unwilling to make concessions. These were set forth in direct appeals to Poland and Czechoslovakia. The new government reassured the Polish people of Germany's sincere desire for lasting reconciliation between the two nations, and it continued to state: ". . . we have not forgotten . . . [Poland's] sorrowful history . . . and we can appreciate . . . more than ever before Poland's desire to live within a state of secured boundaries."[6] The program thus virtually accepted not only the recommendations of the Evangelical and Catholic Churches, but also implied a temporary acceptance of the status quo. That this acceptance should in fact be understood as temporary was carefully stated:

> However, the boundaries of a reunited Germany can only be determined by an agreement, freely arrived at, with an all-German government; an agreement that would establish the preconditions for a good and lasting relationship acceptable to both.[7]

These two statements, taken together, communicate a major change in Bonn's attitude toward Poland. For while the Great

4. "Regierungserklärung . . . ," p. D16.
5. *Loc. cit.*
6. "Regierungserklärung," *op. cit.*, p. D17.
7. *Ibid.*, p. D16.

Coalition still postponed final settlement of German-Polish frontiers until the establishment of a unified German government, the reference to a life "within a state with secured boundaries" was tantamount to an official appreciation that Poland would feel secure only within her present boundaries. This was not the same as the unequivocal recognition of the Oder-Neisse boundary Poland demanded, however, even though indefinite postponement of a final settlement amounted to accepting the status quo. Moreover, even formal recognition of the Oder-Neisse line would have been of little value to Poland unless recognition of the DDR as a sovereign German state were included. Reconciliation between Poland and West Germany was not to be had so easily, as the harsh and hostile reaction of Gomulka's government was to demonstrate.

The Coalition's approach to Czechoslovakia seemed to hold greater promise of success. Ever since the expulsion of the Sudeten-Germans from Czechoslovakia at the end of the Second World War disagreement between the two countries had been focused on the infamous Munich Agreement. The Great Coalition's program acknowledged that the Munich Agreement, reached under duress, was not valid — an acknowledgment which had earlier been made by former Chancellor Erhard. However, all references to the "right to home" (Heimatrecht and Heimatvertriebene) were, for the first time, absent. This omission signaled the end of West Germany's insistence that the Sudeten-Germans had a right to their homeland, a concept which has been interpreted by the expellee-organizations as a "right to return" and once there, a "right to self-determination" with all the ominous implications of both interpretations. Merely by failing to reaffirm the earlier position, the Kiesinger government provided both Bonn and Prague with the badly needed latitude to seek "to end . . . [this] sad chapter in the history of our peoples . . . and to establish a relationship of a neighborhood of confidence."[8]

New Approach to Pankow

While the initiatives taken to improve relations with Poland

8. "Regierungserklärung . . . ," *op. cit.*, p. D17.

and Czechoslovakia were important, nowhere was the desire for a more active and more conciliatory West German foreign policy better illustrated than in the passage of the governmental declaration dealing with East Germany. The Social Democratic conviction that there was a need to align official policy with existing political realities had clearly carried the day. The Coalition program's outline of the basic principles which would govern its dealings with East Germany demonstrated a strong desire both to end the Cold War between Bonn and Pankow, and to conduct this new German policy within the larger framework of the West's search for a general East-West *détente*.

The Coalition's German policy included substantial departures from West Germany's earlier position, and had the East German regime accepted these concessions as a basis for further discussion, it is possible they could have led to a normalization of inter-German relations. To be sure, Bonn's right to "speak for all the German people" was still upheld; but its claim to the "right of sole representation" had been dropped. Earlier stands were further softened by Bonn's assurances that it did not arrogate to itself any right "to hold our kinfolk . . . under its tutelage in the other part of Germany."[9]

The real measure of Bonn's reappraisal of its relations with Pankow, however, was the change in its order of priorities. The Coalition partners had faced the same dilemma as Adenauer before them: whether to give humanitarian considerations greater weight than the elusive goal of national unity, or not. To formulate a new foreign policy which involved a tacit acceptance of another Germany and so officially accepted indefinite postponement of German reunification took no small degree of courage. But in the interests of "promoting the humanitarian, economic, and spiritual [cultural] relationships with our kinfolk . . . with all our power,"[10] the Coalition charted a course intended to smooth rather than exacerbate inter-German relations.

The new policy accepted eventual official contacts of some sort with the Pankow administration. Obviously, such contacts

9. *Ibid.*, p. D17.
10. "Regierungserklärung . . . ," *op. cit.*, p. D16.

could develop into an official recognition of East Germany, and they would in any case be open to interpretation by Pankow or by other states that they constituted recognition. The Coalition program sought to guard against the latter eventuality by stating explicitly that, while Bonn was willing to engage in contacts between the administrative authorities of the other part of Germany, should such a step be warranted by specific issues, none of these contacts would "mean recognition."[11]

The fact that the Coalition's program still clung to the old principle of non-recognition ultimately limited its effectiveness, but for two reasons the decision seemed justified at the time. First, the new government expected that it would be possible, by developing contacts between the two administrations, to prevent further deepening of the *nation's* division, even though the German *state* would remain divided. The West Germans hoped to achieve a "regulated side-by-side existence" of the two German units, even if this process involved direct contacts on and above the administrative level. These moves were to be carried out in coordination with the West's policy of *détente*, moreover, as the new Foreign Minister, Willy Brandt, affirmed in his speech before the Consultative Assembly of the Council of Europe.[12] Second, the new Coalition government hoped that merely by softening its insistence on "exclusive representation" and by proposing steps toward normalization, the Communist accusation that West Germany was bent upon incorporating East Germany within itself would lose credence. Finally, by emphasizing that they sought only to make life more bearable for the Germans in Ulbricht's realm, Bonn expected to alleviate the fears of many East German Communists that regulation of inter-German relations would in fact involve a campaign to de-socialize East German society.

The SPD's Sober Unorthodoxy

The December, 1966, Coalition program was little more than

11. *Ibid.*
12. "Rede des deutschen Bundesminister des Auswärtigen, vor der Beratenden Versammlung des Europarats am 24. Januar, 1967," *Bulletin des Presse- und Informationsamtes der Bundesregierung*, No. 8, January 26, 1967; as to the general attitude of the Consultative Assembly of the Council of Europe, see its *Report on the General Policy of the Council of Europe*, Document No. 2162, January 16, 1967, and its *Resolutions and Recommendations, ibid.*

an outline — a declaration of intentions — and much remained to be explicated in greater detail. Two members of the new government in particular subsequently undertook the task of elaboration, Herbert Wehner, Minister for All-German Affairs, and the new Foreign Minister, Willy Brandt. In interviews given to the domestic and foreign press, in radio messages, and in speeches delivered before the Federal Assembly and other political bodies, both statesmen displayed a willingness to compromise with East Germany that was virtually unprecedented in the Federal Republic.[13] It must have come as a surprise even to those accustomed to Herbert Wehner's almost religious pragmatism to listen to his proposal for the convocation of a Four Power Conference, not to end Germany's division, but to make the status quo bearable. It must have been equally surprising — and not only to the East — to hear proposals for first "freezing" then simultaneously reducing troop levels in both parts of Germany. However, the greatest surprise was Wehner's suggestion that Bonn could re-examine its refusal to recognize the DDR, if the latter adopted the Yugoslav model for socio-political and economic structure.[14] These proposals were most unorthodox by what had previously been official West Germany standards, but by not disassociating himself from Wehner's suggestions, Chancellor Kiesinger gave them the government's stamp of approval.

When Brandt spoke before the Council of Europe on January 24, 1967, he continued to enlarge upon his government's new Eastern policy. He stated his belief that Bonn's policy of relaxation would make a lasting European security arrangement possible, and gave assurances that "a . . . [policy of] relaxation will not be burdened by preconditions" set up by West Germany. He also declared that a "lasting European

13. Interview of Willy Brandt with *Welt am Sonntag* on January 8, 1967, reprinted in the *Bulletin, Presse- und Informationsamtes der Bundesregierung*, No. 3, 1967, pp. 16–17; see also Herbert Wehner's radio message broadcasted by RIAS on January 7, 1967, reprinted in *ibid.*, p. 17. Cf. as representing the consensus within the Coalition "Weitgespannte Politik des Friedens und der Verständigung," Kiesinger's address to the 84th session of the *Bundestag* on January 18, 1967, *Bulletin, Presse- und Informationsamt der Bundesregierung*, No. 6, 1967, pp. 41-42.
14. Theo Sommer, "Politik ohne Gänsefüsschen," *Die Zeit*, February 14, 1967; see also "A German Lead," *Washington Post*, February 2, 1968.

security arrangement will include a reunited Germany."[15] but accepted that this eventual re-establishment of a unitary German state would be toward the end, not the beginning, of the long process of East-West rapprochement. While Brandt soberly warned against unfounded hopes for success, he made it clear that he considered Europe's and West Germany's new approach toward the East a useful tool with which to work for the "adjustment of opposite interests and objectives." He further anticipated that, once the lowest common denominator between Eastern and Western Europe is found, it "could serve as the basis of a lasting European security arrangement."[16]

Cautious though Brandt's optimism was, one must wonder whether — even in the unusually favorable atmosphere of 1967 —it was justified. Not only did the "policy of relaxation" and *détente* have different meanings for Bonn and for the East, within the Western camp itself there were important nuances in the use of these terms. Genuine relaxation meant for Moscow and most of the satellites, the perpetuation of the status quo. It was to be equivalent to legalizing the results of World War II: the division of Germany, and the integration of the DDR into the alliance- and economic-system of the Soviet Union. Moreover, in France, with or without de Gaulle, the settlement of the German problem was not understood to be identical with the re-establishment of a unitary German state. Indeed, relaxation for the French was envisaged as a reduction of tensions between West Germany and the East made possible by the prior acceptance of Germany's division by Bonn, a step that neither Kiesinger, nor Brandt nor Wehner were willing explicitly to undertake.

Furthermore, one must also wonder whether in 1966-7 there was really evidence that the Soviet Union and its allies were themselves in fact ready reciprocally to change their foreign policy postures in any significant way. It is true that during the early and mid-sixties the Kremlin seemed to have abandoned the aggressive methods which had characterized the classical period of the Cold War. It is also true that during the same time period the USSR had demonstrated remarkable

15. "Report of the Consultative Assembly . . . ," *op. cit.*, p. D82.
16. *Loc. cit.*

leniency toward the economic reforms with which some of the East European Communists were experimenting. But it is equally true that at no time during these years did the Soviet Union alter the broad outlines of its foreign policy, nor did it become less despotic domestically. Still less did it give evidence of willingness to engage in talks that might change the status quo in Europe. Kurt London aptly describes Soviet-style "peaceful coexistence" as a coin, one side of which shows the willingness to make adjustments whenever they serve the Soviet purpose, but the other side of which shows consistent pursuit of "ideological warfare on the political, social and economic levels."[17]

Despite the fact that nationalism and the ramifications of the technological revolution had caused Communism in Eastern Europe to undergo an enormous transformation by the mid-sixties, it is important to question whether the fundamental nature of these systems changed. Every social or economic reform has been initiated by communist parties which continue to act not only without domestic institutional restraints, but to subordinate themselves to the preferences of the Kremlin in all important matters. While an indigenous Communist Party may to some extent dictate the pace of change, the Kremlin can employ the tools of "increasing resistance [against] revolutions of rising expectations."[18] as demonstrated in 1953, 1956, and 1968.

Such considerations did not dampen the enthusiasm with which Bonn's Eastern policy was received both in the Federal Republic and in other Western capitals. Observers were nearly unanimous in expressing deep satisfaction and even optimism. Only a few warned against euphoria, and pointed to the enormous difficulties which remained to be surmounted.[19]

17. For a detailed and most convincing analysis of this topic see Kurt London, "Entspannung und Friedensstrategie: Entspannung als Methode oder Endziel?" in Alfred Domes (ed.), *Entspannung, Sicherheit, Frieden* (Verlag Wissenschaft und Politik, Koeln, 1968), pp. 163–78.
18. The phrase was borrowed from James H. Billington, "Force and Counter-force in Eastern Europe," *Foreign Affairs*, Vol. 47, No. 1 (October, 1968), pp. 26–35, one of the best analyses of the situation in Eastern Europe in the light of the Soviet intervention in Czechoslovakia.
19. To this see especially, Heinrich Bechtold, "Kiesinger und die deutsche Aussenpolitik," *Aussenpolitik*, Vol. 17, No. 12, pp. 705–8; among the most noted and most sober newspaper commentators see Hansjakob Stehle, "The

Initial Reactions to the New Policy

Formidable difficulties had to be faced in the practical implementation of Bonn's new Eastern policy. Any diplomatic overture to Eastern Europe would fail if it were interpreted by Moscow as an attempt to undermine its position in the area. Similarly, improvement of Bonn's relations with any of the East European Communist states would be impossible if moves in that direction were understood as an attempt to isolate the DDR. Finally, Kiesinger, Brandt, and their itinerant emissaries had to convince East European regimes that Bonn would not seek normalization or understanding with the Soviet Union at their expense.

Despite such obstacles, announcement of the new Eastern policy elicited positive initial reactions from several Eastern capitals. The most encouraging response came from Bucharest. In Budapest, Hungarian Foreign Minister János Péter declared Hungary's readiness to normalize her relations with the Federal Republic "under suitable circumstances."[20] A Budapest radio commentator praised Bonn's "noteworthy efforts," and expressed the hope that West Germany would readjust to European realities without too much loss of prestige. Budapest, such announcements implied, was willing to cooperate in finding a formula whereby Bonn could re-establish diplomatic relations with Hungary without prior official recognition of the DDR. As one Hungarian newspaper pointed out, Bonn was not a "hopeless case" nor were the obstacles for a normalization of relations between the two countries as fundamental as they were in the case of Poland, Czechoslovakia, and the DDR. Furthermore, it was emphasized that in the light of the traditional, cultural, economic, and even political bonds between the two countries, the absence of normal diplomatic relations constituted an "unnatural state of affairs." Much importance was

Prospects for a new Eastern Policy," *Die Zeit*, December 16, reprinted in *The German Tribune*, No. 247, p. 2. Cf. Marion Graefin Dönhoff, "Ein Anfang ist gemacht," *Die Zeit*, February 7, 1967; Rudolf Zundel, "Gemischte Gefuehle in Bonn," *ibid.*, February 14; Theo Sommer, "Kein Alibi für Nichtstun," *ibid.*, January 14, 1967, and Walter Lippmann, "Too Good to be True?" *Newsweek*, January 30, 1967.

20. *Népszabadság*, December 25, 1966.

attached to Bonn's rapid rapprochement with Paris which was seen in Budapest as a development which would contribute to a genuine relaxation of European tensions. However irrational subsequent events would prove their hopes to be, in 1966 and in early 1967 Hungarian intellectuals and journalists felt recent improvements in Soviet-French and Franco-German relations might set the stage for their country to escape from Soviet tutelage.

While somewhat less positive, Czechoslovak reaction to Bonn's Eastern policy was delivered in an unusually conciliatory tone. Significantly, when West German mass media interpreted an interview by Czech Deputy Foreign Minister Klicka as being absolutely negative,[21] Radio Prague hastened to emphasize the government's willingness for honest compromise with Bonn.[22]

For its part encouraged by such demonstrations of cautious good will, the West German government undertook some intensive political reconnoitering. A delegation from the West German Foreign Ministry held talks in Bucharest between January 7 and 16, and another was sent to Prague for exploratory talks on January 9. A delegation under State Secretary Rolf Lahr went to Budapest to discuss bilateral problems of a non-economic character. Following Lahr's conversations with the Hungarian Foreign Minister and other governmental representatives, a communique was issued stating that, among other topics, the possibilities of establishing diplomatic relations had been explored.[23] As late as January 26 — more than three weeks after Ulbricht unleashed his diplomatic counter-offensive against the Federal Republic — the Hungarian government was still willing to explore the possibility of some sort of compromise with Bonn.

Exploratory talks in Prague were less promising than those in Bucharest and Budapest had been. According to impartial

---

21. "Attitudes Harden in Prague," *Frankfurter Allgemeine Zeitung*, December 22, 1966, reprinted in *The German Tribune*, No. 248, January 7, 1967.
22. "Rundfunkgespräch zwischen dem stellvertretenden tschechoslovakischen Aussenminister Ota Klicka und dem Leiter der aussenpolitischen Redaktion des Tschechoslovakischen Rundfunks, am 20. Dezember, 1966," translation of the original reprinted in *Europa Archiv, Dokumente*, Vol. 22, pp. D99–101.
23. Hansjakob Stehle, "Botschafter nach Budapest?" *Die Zeit*, January 31. 1967.

commentators[24] the greatest stumbling block was agreement on a mutually acceptable formula for the Federal Republic's relationship with West Berlin. Preliminary understandings had been cleared both with Rumania and Hungary when official Trade Missions were established in those countries, but by January, 1967, mounting pressure from East Germany and the Soviet Union had already made speedy agreement impossible. Nevertheless, the Prague conversations were productive in that they left the door open for eventual agreement on the exchange of Trade Missions.

"Active Eastern policy," and "policy of flexibility," the subject of heated political debate for five years, had previously been implemented by "little steps" and cautious maneuvering. The Kiesinger-Brandt-Wehner triumvirate moved to swift and pragmatic action. Former West German Foreign Minister Gerhard Schröder had prepared the diplomatic ground in Eastern Europe, creating favorable conditions for a more elastic Eastern policy. He can be credited with the establishment of Trade Missions in Budapest, Bucharest, Warsaw and Sofia, for example, and since the Missions in Bucharest and Sofia exercised some consular functions, their conversion into diplomatic missions was so much the easier.

Bonn's first tangible result came as early as the end of January. On January 26 the Federal Assembly authorized Brandt to reach an agreement with his Rumanian counterpart on the establishment of diplomatic relations. Corneliu Manescu paid a visit to Bonn between January 30 and February 3, and on February 1 Chancellor Kiesinger reported to the West German Parliament that Bonn and Bucharest had agreed to exchange ambassadors.[25] A major first step in normalizing relations with Eastern Europe was taken, and after almost two decades of hesitation, search, trials, and errors, the Federal Republic re-established political presence in Eastern Europe.

24. "Sondierungen Lahrs in Budapest," *Neue Zürcher Zeitung*, January 24, 1967; "Bonn's Fühler nach dem Osten," *ibid.*, January 26, 1967.
25. "Erklärung des deutschen Bundeskanzlers ver dem Bundestag am 1. Februar 1967 über die Aufnahme diplomatischer Beziehungen zu Rumaenien," *Bulletin der Presse- und Informationsamtes der Bundesregierung*, No. 11, 21 February 1967; see also "Ergebnisse des Besuchs des rumaenischen Aussen-

A Balance Sheet

The establishment of diplomatic relations with Rumania was unquestionably a spectacular success for Bonn. The success was nevertheless a qualified one. It is instructive at this point to draw up a balance sheet as of December, 1966, and January, 1967. On the plus side, Rumania took a step that was vigorously opposed by both the Soviet Union and its influential satellite in East Germany. This was incontrovertible evidence that there had been a loosening of the Communist bloc's former iron discipline and compulsory "socialist solidarity," thus giving rise to renewed optimism.

On the other hand, the mere exchange of ambassadors was in and of itself of limited significance for a variety of reasons. By 1967, after all, Rumania had become notorious for its unorthodoxy in ideological and economic matters and for its resistance to Soviet control. Also, the act of exchanging ambassadors alone did not guarantee further rapprochement of the two countries. Moreover, establishing diplomatic relations with *one* country in Eastern Europe was not a decisive test of Bonn's real political success. Had the Rumanian example been followed by Hungary and Czechoslovakia, for example, Bonn could indeed have been credited with a major political breakthrough. Establishing relations with the renegade Rumanians only, on the other hand, could conceivably have an *adverse* affect between East and West. Conservative politicians inside and outside the Kremlin made increasingly persistent warnings against diplomatic or economic incursions by West Germany in East Europe. It was difficult to predict, as of early 1967, which forces within the communist camp would gain the upper hand.

Warning Signals from Warsaw and Budapest

Ominous signs of reaction among conservative communists could already be discerned in Poland and Hungary as early as the end of 1966. At that time Poland reversed its policy of

Ministers, Corneliu Manescu, in der Bundesrepublik Deutschland vom 31. Januar bis zum 3. February" (Kommuniqué vom 3. Januar), *ibid.*

domestic liberalization and limited national emancipation. Polish intransigence on the boundary question increased, and lapses into the language of the cold war became more frequent. Developments in Hungary were more ambiguous. Between 1962 and 1965 the Party and government, by following a liberal domestic policy, had been able to establish a relationship with the population which could be described as less than fundamental consensus but more than mutual tolerance. A sweeping amnesty freeing most of those condemned after the 1956 revolution, a liberalized passport policy which opened gates toward the West and application in practice of the slogan "whoever is not against us is with us," were but a few indications of Hungary's relative domestic tranquillity. During the same period the formulation and conduct of Hungarian foreign policy was carefully designed to be congruent with a genuine relaxation of worldwide tensions.

The combined effects of economic stagnation and of rising expectations gradually brought the halcyon years of the early sixties to an end in Hungary. A pervasive sense of malaise spread both within Party and government and in the population at large. Among other things, the number of "legal defectors" — Hungarians who failed to return to the country after a visit to the West — increased somewhat, particularly among professionals. Official Hungarian reaction was a self-defeating series of repressive measures which only fed the disillusionment whose outward signs it sought to quell. General nervousness about the stability of the domestic scene almost certainly helps account for Hungary's equivocal response to West Germany's new Eastern policy.

While the Hungarian government seemed willing to explore possibilities for compromise with Bonn as late as January, 1967, Kádár had taken an unmistakably hard line in an address to the Hungarian Party Congress the previous month. He specifically accused West Germany of harboring "subversive, espionage, and terroristic organizations which are directed against Eastern Europe" and which "poison the whole European atmosphere."[26] He went on to declare that Bonn could not expect rapproche-

26. *Népszabadság*, December 29, 1966.

ment with East Europe as long as these organizations continued to exist, thus articulating Hungary's first pre-condition for normalization of German-Hungarian relations. Perhaps most significantly, Kádár stated that "political understanding with the Federal Republic cannot be brought about on a purely bilateral basis."[27] The implication that the German question must be treated as a common concern of the whole Eastern Bloc was clear. His emphasis on the protective role of "proletarian internationalism" against the "destructive forces of egotistic nationalism" signalled the beginning of the end of an era of relative freedom from overbearing Soviet influence.

The Hungarian Communist Party's new trend toward increasing bloc-solidarity was not immediately reflected in the Hungarian government's response to West Germany's new overtures. While the Hungarian Foreign Minister did say that normalization of relations would depend on Bonn's willingness to accept the existence of the two German states as a reality, by not making official recognition of the DDR a *sine qua non* of rapprochement between the two countries he left the door open for further negotiation.

By January, 1967, then, West Germany's new coalition government had enjoyed some obviously important if limited success in some East European capitals. Whether these would lead to the re-establishment of Germany's political presence in East-Central Europe, the opening of markets with increasing demands for Western credits and technical know-how to West Germany, the gradual disappearance of deepseated suspicion of German motives in the area, or ultimately to the reunification of the two Germanies was far from obvious, however. The key

27. Kádár's quoted statement represented a further elaboration on the same theme which was discussed earlier in an interview given to the UPI correspondent Henry Shapiro. In this interview Kádár placed great emphasis on the "overall interests of the Socialist community" as contrasted to those of the individual Socialist (Communist) states. To this see: *Népszabadság*, August 2, 1966. For a full, but somewhat edited version see *Wissenschaftlicher Dienst Südosteuropa*, No. 7, 1966. It is of further interest to note that the same concept was discussed even earlier by one of the members of the Central Committee of the Hungarian Communist Party, Zoltan Komocsin, who pleaded for increased "internationalist solidarity" in an article entitled "Patriotism, National Interests, Internationalism" in *Problems of Freedom and Socialism*, June 10, 1966, pp. 11–19.

to the future success of the new policies lay, events were soon to demonstrate, in the Kremlin.

5

ulbricht
and eastern europe

Citizen and Government in East Germany

Germany, a nation divided into two separate states, is a major theater of East-West ideological struggle. It is commonplace in the West to speak of the eastern part of Germany as the last bastion of stalinism and of its relationship to Moscow as that of the most subservient satellite — and still largely accurate. However, East Germany under Walter Ulbricht has succeeded where its communist-run neighbors have all failed, namely, in the spectacularly successful establishment of a modern industrial economy. Today East German industry ranks second only to that of the USSR among communist states. Its production is indispensable to the economic development of Eastern Europe, and it has become an important presence on the international market, particularly as a supplier to the underdeveloped nations. Moreover, far from being the kind of static political system usually associated with authoritarian rule, economic success and other factors have set in motion a process which is changing relations between government and its citizenry in intriguing and unexpected ways.

Thoughtful observers of East German society have noted that the population at large has become significantly less hostile

toward the government in recent years. Its socialist achievements — low housing costs, an efficient medical benefit plan,
and free education — have come to be appreciated. Land reform and the socialization of the industries have been accepted
or even applauded. Moreover, a new "Germanness,"[1] a state
of mind which does not necessarily reject the idea of the "two
Germanies," has gradually emerged. In short, East Germans,
with many individual reservations, have slowly moved beyond
mere toleration to acccept the flourishing communist state
under which they live.[2]

It is basically irrelevant whether or not this new relationship
between the state and its citizens should be attributed to the
fact that it was East Germany where many of the good characteristics of the Prussian mentality[3] survived, or to the Berlin
Wall which forced the citizen to accept the inescapable, or to
pride of achievement in a most adverse situation. What is
relevant is the fact that the majority of the East German population goes beyond mere toleration of the state, and while the
degree of its loyalty may be questioned, the practical disappearance of outright hostility toward the regime must be
considered as another stabilizing factor behind the Berlin
Wall.[4]

1. For an early account on the changing attitudes and their sources see the
series of articles which appeared in the *New York Times*, April 18–21, 1966;
see also Jean Edward Smith, "Our View of a Stagnated East Germany is
Dated," *The Washington Post*, April 16, 1967, p. C2; another but slightly
different appraisal of East Germany's domestic development can be found in
Peter Frigge's "Bürger, Staat und Regime in der DDR", *Neue Zürcher
Zeitung*, April 29, 1967.
2. One of the leading experts on the problem of German reunification also
discusses the relationship between the citizen and the East German state in
the most enlightening analysis, but comes to somewhat different conclusions.
See Ferenc A. Váli, *The Quest for a United Germany* (The Johns Hopkins
Press, Baltimore, 1967), pp. 173 ff.
3. See Marion Graefin Doenhoff, "Vorbild Preussen?" *Die Zeit*, February
21, 1967.
4. However, the allegiance of the East German population should not be
overestimated. At the present it is impossible to give an accurate estimate of
the real impact of the following factors on this emerging trend: resignation,
opportunism, cynicism, and/or honest conviction. It seems to the author that
the degree of acceptance has yet to be tested, and it is entirely conceivable
that if today the barriers dividing the two parts of Germany should be
demolished, the exodus of thousands would immediately follow.

The relationship between the individual and the regime is still uneasy, however, and it is at the very least premature to speak about "the enthusiasm the System has aroused."[5] Significant and occasionally vocal dissent has come, just as in the Soviet Union, from intellectuals and from scholars in the natural sciences. The DDR's provincial intellectual life and the Party's impossible demand that scientific work be tailored to ideological guidelines have provoked special criticism. The new generation of technocrats similarly finds it difficult to identify with the Ulbricht regime, and has been unable to reconcile the requirements of modern technology with the postulates of Communist ideology.[6] Social scientists have also chafed under the East German Party's intellectual tutelage, and for its part, the regime has not hesitated to purge recalcitrant faculty and students from time to time. Dissent within the East German intellectual elite hampers the regime's attempts at further political consolidation, but even in these circles credit is given for its economic achievements.

Ulbricht's Diplomatic Counteroffensive

While in early 1967 the East German regime was thus able to view its domestic political situation with some satisfaction, its position within the Communist bloc was rather precarious. The energy and skill with which the West German government initiated its new Eastern policy caused considerable alarm. It seemed evident to the Ulbricht government that a stable West German political presence in Eastern Europe, accompanied by industrial penetration of the markets there and eventual projection of a new German image, could seriously undermine the DDR's position in the area. The fact that the Western policy was to be synchronized with the overall objectives of the United

5. Jean E. Smith, *op. cit.*, p. A5.
6. The development of similar anti-ideological sentiments was observed by the author in Hungary in 1968, where not only the technocrats regard Communist ideology as wholly inadequate and inapplicable to modern scientific requirements, but also a considerable part of the disillusioned student body at the universities. See also, Billington, *op. cit.*, p. 33, and for similar tendencies in the Soviet Union: Dimitry Pospielkovsky, "Geistige und politische Auswirkungen der Sowjetischen Wirtschaftsreform," *Osteuropa*, Vol. 18, No. 2 (February, 1968), pp. 96–111, and *passim*.

States,[7] with those of the North Atlantic Treaty Organization,[8] and with those of the Council of Europe made it seem even more ominous.

Response from the Ulbricht regime to Great Coalition Eastern policy was swift, uncompromising and vicious — more uncompromising by far than the reaction from Moscow. The counteroffensive against Bonn sought first to strengthen East Germany's position within the socialist commonwealth by establishing a united front against West Germany within it: more than anything else, East German leaders dreaded political isolation within East Europe. They had at all costs to avoid any accusation from their allies that they were prepared to sacrifice Rumanian, Hungarian or Czech interests to their own. The second objective of East Germany's counteroffensive was simultaneously to deepen the cleavage between the two parts of an already deeply divided nation through political and administrative measures.

The East Berlin *Deutschlandsender* launched a tirade against the Coalition's *détente* policy on the same day that the Kiesinger government presented its new program to the Federal Assembly. The broadcast characterized Bonn's new approach toward Eastern Europe and the German question as "typical of the inertia of Bonn's policy in clinging to the old, unrealistic, and illusory positions."[9] A few days later an article in the official organ of the SED[10] unleashed a personal attack on Willy Brandt. These early reactions were but mild foretastes of the diplomatic offensive that followed. To the apparent surprise and certain dismay of East Germany, Czechoslovakia, Hungary and Rumania had not reacted at all enthusiastically to the idea of establishing a "united front" against Bonn.[11] While neither

7. See "The Outlook for Freedom," address by Dean Rusk, *Department of State Bulletin*, Vol. LV, No. 1425, October 17, 1966, pp. 586–90; see also "Making Europe a Whole: An Unfinished Task," address by President Lyndon B. Johnson, *ibid.*, Vol. LV, No. 1426, October 24, 1966, pp. 622–5.
8. Twelfth Annual Conference of NATO Parliamentarians, November 14–19, Paris. Reports, Resolutions, Recommendations, *NATO, International Secretariat* (Paris, 1966), *passim*.
9. Foreign Broadcast Information Service, December 15, 1966, p. EE1.
10. See *Neues Deutschland*, December 20, 1966.
11. "Bemühungen Pankows um eine Kommunistische Aktionsfront," *Neue Zürcher Zeitung*, January 2, 1967; also "Umgekehrte Hallstein Doktrin,"

Prague nor Budapest may have been seriously considering taking immediate advantage of Bonn's proposals, a strong "united front" under Ulbricht's leadership would automatically put the political and economic gains to be had from closer relations with West Germany beyond their reach for the foreseeable future.

Six months earlier at the July, 1966, Bucharest summit conference of Warsaw Pact countries Ulbricht had insisted unsuccessfully that West German recognition of the DDR be made a pre-condition by every East European country for any further normalization of West German-East European relations. The Warsaw Pact countries apparently agreed only to urge Bonn to "accept the existence of two German states," to "respect the existing boundaries in Europe," and "to refrain from possession or co-possession of nuclear weapons."[12] In his December 15 speech to the Central Committee of the SED, however, Ulbricht asserted that the Bucharest Declaration contained "obligatory principles for all the fraternal socialist countries"[13] in their dealing with the German problem. Ulbricht again demanded that no East European state normalize relations with West Germany until the latter first recognized the German Democratic Republic. By making those declarations at a time when for all practical purposes the Bonn Coalition had abandoned the Hallstein Doctrine,[14] the East German government served notice that it would answer Bonn's every concession with an increase in its own demands.[15] And

ibid., January 8, 1967.
12. "Erklärung der Teilnehmerstaaten des Warschauer Vertrags vom 6. Juli 1966 zur europäischen Sicherheit," *Neues Deutschland*, July 7, 1966, reprinted in *Europa Archiv*, Vol. 21, pp. D414–24.
13. See *Neues Deutschland*, December 16, 1966.
14. The question whether or not the "Ulbricht Doctrine" would be as inflexible, and as successful in its application as the Hallstein Doctrine had been was an open one at that time. However, in the light of the last three years' experience it is possible to say that whereas it proved to be more or less effective with regard to most of the East European states (although its impact should not be overestimated), the attitude of the non-committed nations toward both Germanies remained basically unchanged.
15. The increase in Ulbricht's demands even for an exploratory dialogue between Bonn and East Berlin about the possibilities of a German confederation could be best seen in comparing the contents of his New Year's message

indeed, in a New Year's message addressed to the entire German population, Ulbricht rejected outright the idea of the country's reunification "under the prevailing circumstances."[16] He also announced a ten-point program of pre-conditions for the realization of "even a confederation between East and West Germany." It was virtually certain that some of these ten points would be impossible for any West German government to accept: recognition of the DDR, establishment of diplomatic relations between Bonn and East Berlin, a guarantee of the DDR's boundaries and the establishment of a joint commission empowered to inquire in both parts of Germany whether or not the Potsdam stipulations concerning the guarantees for democracy in Germany had been faithfully executed.[17] Given the grim history of joint East-West commissions in Germany since the war, this last condition must surely have been offered in bad faith.

For those in Bonn who had believed it possible to enter into a dialogue on rapprochement with East Germany, Ulbricht's message[18] must have been a great disappointment. As one West German newspaper said, "the lord and master of the other part of Germany made his ambition more obvious than ever: division of Germany once and for all into two German states."[19] However, Ulbricht's stubbornness, encouraged by Moscow and probably by Warsaw,[20] did not mean that he was acting from a position of strength. Quite the contrary. The East German regime's frantic diplomatic activity in the capitals of the "fraternal" socialist countries was a demonstration of the depth of Ulbricht's concern.

---

of 1967 with his address delivered at the twentieth anniversary of the establishment of the SED. See "Rede des Vorsitzenden des Staatsrats und Ersten Sekretär der SED am 21. April 1966 in Berlin," *Neues Deutschland*, April 22, 1966. Cf. "Neujahrsbotschaft 1965 . . . ," *op. cit.*, p. D95.

16. See "Neujahrsbotschaft des Staatsratsvorsitzenden der DDR, Walter Ulbricht, vom December 31, 1966," *Aussenpolitische Korrespondenz*, Ost Berlin, January 7, 1967, reprinted in excerpts in *Europa Archiv*, Vol. 22, pp. D102–4.

17. *Ibid.*, p. D104.

18. See *Neues Deutschland*, January 16, 19, 20, 1967.

19. *Christ und Welt*, January 6, 1967.

20. To this see: Brezhnev's speech at Gorki on January 13, 1967, and Rapacki's interview with *Tribuna Ludu* on December 31, 1966, the former given in excerpts in *Europa Archiv*, Vol. 22, pp. D104–6.

Early Search for Bloc-solidarity

In early 1967 Ulbricht had every reason to be concerned. The reactions of Prague, Budapest, and Bucharest to Bonn's overtures were deliberately vague and cautiously formulated and they showed reluctance in these capitals to allow East Germany to be sole arbiter of the German question. The East German regime first concentrated on soliciting support for increased bloc-solidarity in Moscow and Warsaw, and after some hesitation the Kremlin came to Ulbricht's aid. There were increased contacts between high-level political and military representatives and much-publicized negotiations on further strengthening economic coordination between the two countries. Moreover, Otto Winzer, the Foreign Minister of East Germany, was permitted to publish his government's views in *Pravda*, a gesture tantamount to endorsement, and a clear warning to recalcitrant members of the bloc.

These contacts were supplemented by conversations between the East German and the Polish Foreign Ministers, which took place only a few days before the Bonn-Bucharest rapprochement became a matter of public record and before the beginning of Bonn's exploratory discussions in Prague and Budapest as well. The Poles feared that if Budapest and Prague should follow Bucharest, Poland would find herself more or less isolated in the company of Ulbricht. Yet in spite of Polish uneasiness on this score, there was a limit beyond which Gomulka and his Foreign Minister were unwilling to go.

Polish reluctance to follow the East German line without reservations was clearly visible during Rapacki's visit to Paris at the end of January. The official reason for his conversations in Paris was to promote Franco-Polish economic cooperation, but references to the Eastern question were made in various addresses and interviews by both Rapacki and Couve de Murville.[21] And at Rapacki's press conference on January 27, he outlined his government's position with regard to Bonn's policy of relaxation. He reiterated longstanding Polish demands for normalization of Polish-German relations, but

21. See *New York Times*, January 29, 1967; *Die Welt*, January, 29, 30, 31, 1967; also Couve de Murville's interview with *Le Figaro*, February 1, 1967.

differed from Ulbricht on one extremely important point: Bonn's recognition of the DDR was not made a necessary precondition for rapprochement with Poland in particular or with Central Europe in general. "The establishment of formal relations with Bonn is a private affair of every [socialist] state,"[22] he declared. Deliberate use of the word "formal", implying that Poland was willing to differentiate between "formalized" and "normalized" diplomatic relations, left the door open for further political bargaining. And in referring to establishment of relations as a private affair, Rapacki delineated the limits beyond which Poland would be reluctant to follow Ulbricht.

Clearly, as of January, the East German position was not receiving the support it needed to be successful in any of the other East European bloc countries that had been approached by West Germany. Ulbricht set about ruthlessly to subordinate his allies' interests to those of his regime, and to institutionalize this subordination in a manner which would render it permanent. To this end, during the spring of 1967 the East Germans saw to it that Moscow called conferences on the highest governmental and party levels to re-establish bloc-solidarity and they concluded a series of bilateral treaties with other East European states designed to strengthen East Germany's position in Eastern Europe. The first of these communist summit conferences was held in Warsaw between February 8 and 10.

Immediately prior to the Warsaw Foreign Ministers' Conference, East Germany's party newspaper delivered an attack on Rumania[23] deploring not only that country's rapprochement with West Germany, which by that time had already become official, but also Bucharest's lack of consideration for East Germany's position in this matter. This heavy-handed move, identified by the Rumanians as "unjustified interference in domestic affairs," compromised in advance East Germany's prospects for success.[24]

The brevity of the communiqué issued at Warsaw[25] and its

22. "Rapacki in Paris," *Neue Zürcher Zeitung*, January 27, 1967; also "Rapackis Pariser Gespraeche," *ibid.*, January 30, 1967.
23. *Neues Deutschland*, February 3, 1967.
24. See *Scinteia*, February 5, 1967.
25. "Kommuniqué über die Konferenz der Aussenminister der Mitgliedstaaten des Warschauer Paktes," *Europa Archiv*, Vol. 22, pp. D123-4.

concluding words saying that "the consultations were conducted in an . . . atmosphere of . . . *mutual understanding*" [italics added] speak for themselves. The main issue at Warsaw had been whether or not the members of the Warsaw Pact would be obliged to consult with Pankow *prior* to engaging in political conversations with Bonn.[26] While elevation of the Bucharest Declaration to doctrine may have been acceptable to the Pact members, accepting compulsory consultations with Pankow would have been equivalent to granting a veto power to Ulbricht throughout East Europe in matters pertaining to Germany. Such an agreement would have constituted a permanent danger of East German infringement upon the sovereignty of its socialist neighbors, and it is not surprising that the Warsaw meeting ended with an agreement to disagree.

Ulbricht's unexpected fiasco unmistakably demonstrated a degree of polycentrism in Eastern Europe which eventually became intolerable to the Soviet Union. The issue at the Warsaw Conference of 1967 was neither Rumania *versus* East Germany, nor was it Rumania *versus* the USSR; it was a contest between the principle of bloc-solidarity and the dictates of national interest.[27]

East Germany had not, however, exhausted its efforts to bring reluctant members of the socialist camp closer to its own position. Before March, 1967, East Germany's bilateral Friendship and Assistance Pact was that concluded with the USSR on June 12, 1964. The conclusion of Friendship and Mutual Assistance Pacts by East Germany with Poland on March 15, with Czechoslovakia on March 17 and with Hungary on May 18[28] signaled a revitalization of the bilateral alliance system which had bound the East European states to each other and to

Note the difference between the Russian (TAAS in German, February 10, 1967), and the East German (*Neues Deutschland*, February 10, 1967) texts of the communiqué, the latter saying that "the consultations were conducted in *complete agreement*," In Communist terminology there is a basic difference between the two wordings.

26. To this see "Keine Beseitigung der Differenzen in Warschau," *Neue Zürcher Zeitung*, February 11, 1967.

27. Heinrich Bechtold, "Ulbrichts Niederlage in Osteuropa," *Aussenpolitik*, Vol. 18, No. 3 (March, 1967), pp. 129–32.

28. For the original text of these treaties see *Neues Deutschland*, March 16, 1967, and *ibid.*, March 18, 1967.

Moscow ever since the late 1940's.[29] The original Pacts, to which the East Germans had not been party, had been concluded in 1947 and 1948 for twenty year and had pledged cooperation in the event of armed conflict with Germany as a whole. In the new agreements the same clause was extended to armed attack unleashed by "West German militarism and revanchism" or to any other state or group of states in alliance with Bonn.[30]

For all their bellicose language, these Pacts were only a qualified success to Ulbricht's credit. There were significant differences among the three bilateral agreements in the specifications of the reasons for alliance, the guarantee of boundaries and the pre-conditions for normalization of relations between the two halves of Europe. It is sufficient here to note that Poland alone agreed to all the points East Germany sought to include. In contrast, Czechoslovakia and Hungary made do with generalizations concerning the reasons for the alliance and with flexible statements regarding recognition, boundaries, and the problem of West Berlin's special status.[31]

Such reservations notwithstanding, as of late spring, 1967, Ulbricht's diplomatic offensive did seem to have taken some of the initiative away from West Germany's innovative coalition government. A special relationship of sorts had been institutionalized between East Germany and Poland, East Germany and Czechoslovakia and East Germany and Hungary. The East German position had been significantly strengthened by a "compulsory consultation" clause in the Pact with Poland, and weaker but similar wording in the agreement with Czechoslovakia. Although Ulbricht failed to become the sole arbiter of the German question in East Europe, he had unquestionably made progress in that direction. And there can be no doubt but that the pacts would have a certain important deterrent effect on any future attempts by Poland, Czechslovakia,

29. An excellent short analysis of these Pacts is contained in Hans Heinrich Mahnke's "Die Deutschland-Frage in den Freundschafts- und Beistands-Pakten der DDR mit Polen und der CSSR," *Europa Archiv*, Vol. 22, No. 9 (May 10, 1967), pp. 323-8.
30. Mahnke, "Die Deutschland-Frage . . . ," *op. cit.*, p. 323.
31. *Ibid.*, pp. 324 ff.

Hungary, or other bloc countries to normalize relations with West Germany.

Ulbricht's new alliance system also had a number of built-in weaknesses, not the least of which were: resentment among his allies over the strong-arm tactics used to get them to agree to the terms of the new Friendship and Mutual Assistance Pacts; their anxiety about the added handicap being cut off from West Germany would impose on already shaky economies; and uneasiness in Moscow over the possibility that these developments would accentuate the division between the northern tier and the southern tier of East European communist states. Some of these tensions came to the surface during and after the Karlovy Vary Conference of the European Communist Parties held in Czechoslovakia.

The Conference had been planned to discuss problems of European security long before West Germany initiated its dramatic new Eastern policy, but the specific questions to which the conferees were to address themselves — conditions under which a European collective security system could be established and the creation of a communist-directed mass movement to marshall support for accepting these conditions throughout Europe — were themselves more than tangentially related to the German question. Given the time at which the Conference convened, however, it could hardly have avoided serious discussion of how to seize the diplomatic initiative from Bonn.

Stripped to essentials, the Declaration[32] issued at Karlovy Vary called for nothing less than unconditional acceptance of the status quo, including the "finality of all European boundaries" and the "recognition of the existence of two sovereign and equal German states."[33] Nuclear-free zones in Central and Northern Europe, in the Balkans and in the Mediterranean were proposed, but without specifying guarantees which would make them acceptable. A proposal to abolish all military bases on foreign territories was advanced as another feasible step

---

32. "Erklärung für den Frieden und die Sicherheit in Europa," *Neues Deutschland*, April 27, 1967; reprinted in *Europa Archiv*, Vol. 22, pp. D259–66.
33. *Ibid.*, p. 262.

toward a "Europe without tensions."[34] The main condition for
a normalized Europe would be, "a Europe without military
blocs."[35] In this manner the Karlovy Vary Declaration implied support for the simultaneous dismemberment of both
NATO and of the Warsaw Pact, and in this respect it went well
beyond Khruschev's repeated proposals for a non-aggression
pact between the two military systems. It even went beyond
the 1966 Bucharest Declaration, which envisaged the possibility of bilateral agreements between the individual members
of both defense systems.[36]

It is difficult to judge blueprints for hypothetical future worlds,
particularly when they are advanced with a minimum of
practical detail, or to know to what extent they should be taken
at face value. But if the proposal to abolish NATO and the
Warsaw Pact meant that the latter would be replaced by the
crisscrossing bilateral alliances and mutual assistance pacts
which now bind the East European states to each other and to
the Soviet Union, then it was at best deceptive. For dismemberment of the North Atlantic Treaty Organization would not only
involve the abolition of the Western defense system, but also
the disengagement of the United States (as contrasted with the
Soviet Union) from the military affairs of Europe. The "normalized, relaxed and tension-free" Europe envisaged at
Karlovy Vary seems to have been a conglomeration of small
and middle-sized states living in a happy togetherness under
the shadow of the Soviet colossus which would retain virtual
control over the affairs of its immediate neighbors and, unrestrained by the presence of the United States on the European
continent, would extend its sphere of influence to some degree
into Western Europe. It is obvious that the West could not
seriously be expected to pay such an outlandishly high price
for "normalization," if normalization is in fact the appropriate
word.

Indeed, many of the East European signatories of the Declaration of Karlovy Vary were themselves greatly displeased by the
Soviet Union's use of the alleged need to establish a "united

34. *Ibid.*, p. D263.
35. *Loc. cit.*
36. See "Erklärung (Bucharest) . . . ," *op. cit.*, pp. D424 ff.

front" on these matters at the Conference as a means of bringing the semi-autonomous policies of Rumania, Hungary and Czechoslovakia into line. The USSR and East Germany characterized the Conference as a ground-breaking event.[37] While the unanimous adoption of Declarations and Resolutions by the heads of ruling communist parties no longer guarantees that they will be conscientiously implemented, the East German and Soviet moves to block Bonn's new Eastern policy were successful in the middle run. They definitely dampened the enthusiasm of some of the East European countries for more normal political relations with the Federal Republic. But even if the initial pace of relaxation had lost its momentum, it is imperative to remember that the new approaches of such countries as Czechoslovakia and Hungary toward a political solution did not exclude the possibility, remote as it may have been, of a limited political understanding between themselves and Bonn.[38] And even more important, they signaled the beginning of a harder political line in Eastern Europe, one which forced Bonn in turn to revise some aspects of its newly formulated position, and in particular to seek more direct contacts with the other Germany.

37. With regard to the question of unanimity and the problem of submitting to Soviet leadership in matters of foreign policy, see especially Ceausescu's article in *Scinteia*, May 7, 1967, which defends the principle of complete independence of every Communist Party in its decisions in internal and external matters. Although Ceausescu acknowledged the validity of basic Communist principles as well as their obligatory character on every Communist Party, he also maintained that they must recede into the background when confronted with the immediate demands of national interest of the individual Communist state. It is of further interest to note that in 1967 the Rumanian Party leader considered the interference of any other Communist Party in the matters of another as an impermissible anachronism. Cf. Zoltán Komőcsin's article in *Népszabadság*, May 10, 1967, defending the same theses although with much less aggressiveness than Ceausescu. See, also, the resolutions of the Hungarian National Assembly, *Magyar Közlöny*, July 21, 1967.
38. The desire to keep the lines of communication open was most clearly expressed by the President of the Hungarian Council of Ministers (Prime Minister) Jeno Fock, and by his Foreign Minister János Péter during the Hungarian Parliament's debate on foreign policy. While both announcements demonstrated a definite hardening toward Bonn in their adherence to the Karlovy Vary Declaration, at the same time they mentioned the possibility of bilateral agreements of limited political scope with the Federal Republic. See: *Magyar Távirati Iroda*, July 14, 1967.

In sum, then, as of the spring of 1967, Ulbricht's political counter-offensive had been moderately successful. The East German regime had strengthened its position both within Eastern Europe and *vis-à-vis* the Federal Republic. Encouraged by these developments, Ulbricht turned to direct attacks on the West German government.

6

the cold war between bonn and pankow

The history of international relations is replete with examples of divided nations, yet, although they speak the same language and share the same cultural heritage, one would have to search for a long time to find an instance in which the psychological rift is as deep as that between the two parts of divided Germany. The governments of both Germanies must be held responsible for this deplorable state of affairs: both the *immobilisme* and calculated ignorance of the Adenauer era in the West and the unremitting hostility of the Ulbricht regime in the East have fed bitterness and mutual alienation. The timid overtures of the Erhard government did little to change this pattern. Not until the innovative Kiesinger-Brandt Eastern policy did any German government advance proposals which could serve as even a modest beginning toward the eventual lessening of tensions between East and West Germany.

The East German regime had motives in addition to political antipathy per se for prolonging the bitter stand-off. Ulbricht and his aides had excellent reasons to believe that political continuity of the most minimal sort might be impossible to maintain in the DDR, should rapprochement between the two Germanies take place. Only states with secure historical identities can weather the clash of divergent ideologies and diverse socio-political forces and emerge intact. France and Poland, Italy and Hungary, or Britain and Rumania would remain essentially the same nation-states even if their form of government or their socio-political structure should change abruptly. But would East Germany? Most observers, and apparently East German party and government leaders themselves, think not.

The East German leadership gave every sign of understanding perfectly well that a Europe without serious international tensions would rob the East German state of its very *raison d'être.* In the mid-sixties, the West's search for genuine *détente* and Bonn's policy of relaxation were accompanied by an increasingly animated discussion all over Eastern Europe about the inevitability of socio-political changes and about the absolute necessity of a closer East-West economic cooperation. The Ulbricht regime rose to the challenge from 1967 on by taking any and all measures at its disposal to reverse these threatening developments.

From late 1966 on, by contrast, the West German government began to supplement the general guidelines of its new German policy with practical propositions. When even the most uncontroversial direct proposals from Bonn were rejected outright, the Coalition proceeded with a unilateral discussion of the German question in hopes of finding an acceptable point of departure for a dialogue. During the first three months of 1967 a multitude of interviews, announcements, addresses on radio and television and news conferences were given by the three leading members of the new Bonn cabinet.[1] Most of these

1. Chancellor Kiesinger's announcement to the *Bundestag* on January 8, as well as Willy Brandt's and Herbert Wehner's inverviews on January 7 and 8 have already been quoted in footnote 13, Chapter 4. For other speeches and interviews see: Kiesinger's speech entitled, "Für eine dauerhafte und gerechte europäische Friedensordnung," *Bulletin*, No. 10, January 31, 1967, pp. 73-74; see also Kiesinger's interview with the *Deutschlandfunk*, "Der Politik der Gewaltlosigkeit Überzeugungskraft verleihen," *Bulletin*, No. 12, February 8, 1967, pp. 89-91. Cf. Willy Brandt's interview with the Norwegian newspaper *Arbeiderbladet* on February 4, reprinted in the *Bulletin*, No. 13, February 10, 1967, pp. 97-98; Kiesinger's speech "Entschlossenes und Konsequentes Handeln der Regierung," *ibid.*, No. 22, March 1, 1967, pp. 173-5; and Kiesinger's interview on German television, "Aktive Aussen- und Innenpolitik," *ibid.*, No. 29, March 21, 1967, pp. 233-4.

elaborated in rather general terms either on the need for European reconciliation or on West Germany's determination to contribute to the building of a Europe without tensions. Yet in all of these official and semi-official announcements one could clearly discern a sense of urgency about beginning talks directly with the DDR.[2]

During March and April very cautious attempts were made to re-formulate West Germany's claim to the "right of sole representation," so long a major bone of contention between the separate parts of Germany and between Bonn and Moscow as well. Both the Chancellor and his Foreign Minister tried to present this controversial issue in a new light during the Federal Assembly sessions in Berlin in early March.[3] While Kiesinger mainly reiterated his earlier statements, Brandt took pains to modify the substance of the controversy at one of his press conferences. Although he did emphasize that West Germany was not prepared to jettison this basic principle entirely, he nevertheless pointed out that Bonn's claim to exclusive representation should be understood not as a political right but as an obligation on its part. Both Brandt and the Chancellor emphasized that the principle of sole representation did not imply eventual tutelage of Bonn over the other part of Germany so much as it was meant to remind the East German population that it too is an active factor with a rightful voice of its own in the German equation. Then in late March, Herbert Wehner weakened the specifically political implications of this claimed "right" even further by characterizing it as the political articulation of Bonn's *moral obligation* toward those Germans to whom participation in the democratic political process has been denied.[4]

This cautious reinterpretation of the "right of sole representation" was more — and thus less — than just a conciliatory

2. See especially Kiesinger's interview with the *Berliner Morgenpost*, on March 5, 1967, "Berlin als Brücke zwischen West and Ost," *Bulletin*, No. 24, March 5, 1967, pp. 191–2, and Wehner's address in the *Norddeutsche Rundfunk*, "Deutsche Vorschläge zu friedenssichernden Massnahmen," *ibid.*, No. 31, March 29, 1967, pp. 249–50.
3. "Aktive Ostpolitik der Bundesregierung," *Bulletin*, No. 26, March 14, 1967, pp. 208, *passim*.
4. "Deutschlandpolitik im Zeichen der Entspannung," *Neue Zürcher Zeitung*, April 2, 1967, p. 5.

gesture toward the DDR, however. It was also intended to provide an escape clause for any East European states which still hoped to normalize or formalize their relations with the Federal Republic. But ambiguous as this initial gesture may have been, the fact remains that by mid-April the Coalition began to prepare for initiating more intensive contacts with the communist regime in Pankow.

The first formal set of concrete proposals was presented to the East German regime by Chancellor Kiesinger on April 12 in the form of a governmental declaration to the West German Parliament.[5] Since Kiesinger's announcement came only a few days before the opening of the Party Congress of the SED, one may assume that he hoped to exercise some influence over its outcome. Kiesinger's proposals touched on humanitarian, economic, and technological-cultural questions, but above all they were a plea — a plea for increasing contacts between the separated parts of Germany's population. Kiesinger's call for closer economic and technical cooperation between the separated parts of a formerly homogeneous economic unit, for increased cultural exchange and for freer, more frequent contacts among the German youth were the words of a statesman earnestly concerned not only about the future of the Federal Republic but also about the future of the entire German nation.

The Coalition government's declaration also implicitly proposed changes in the status quo which would have been directly advantageous to East Germany. The idea of closer economic cooperation implied increased trade, which in turn implied the extension of credits so badly needed by East Germany. The rationalization of intra-German payments, exchange of technological know-how, increased energy exchange, and a joint effort at improving the lines of traffic communication would be certain to further East Germany's economic development. Last but not least, following through on even a few of Kiesinger's proposals would mean establishing some sort of intra-German political machinery, which would have to be composed of rather high-ranking government officials and experts; and this in turn would be a major step

5. "Erklärung der deutschen Bundesregierung zur Deutschlandpolitik," *Bulletin*, No. 38, April 14, 1967.

toward de facto recognition of the East German government by the Federal Republic.

The outcome of the East Germany Party Congress was awaited with some degree of optimism. *Die Zeit* wrote: "When the final curtain drops on the SED's seventh Congress observers will only begin to speculate on the future direction of Ulbricht's foreign policy."[6] The Swiss newspaper *Neue Zürcher Zeitung* speculated whether or not Ulbricht would be pressed to abandon his "all or nothing" policy, even if for tactical purposes.[7] But optimism soon proved to be premature, for although the Kiesinger initiative created some confusion among the SED's leaders, Bonn's attempt to soften the East German stand came to nought.

In April, 1967, Ulbricht gave a speech at the Party Congress entitled "Social Progress in the DDR until the fulfillment of Socialism."[8] In it he purported to see an "increased imperialist aggressiveness, a tightening of international tensions and a more immediate danger of war"[9] in Europe, but he went on to add in almost the same breath that "certain trends towards relaxation in Europe are unmistakable," a position which required no mean analytical sleight of hand. Ulbricht continued in the same vein, saying that "Bonn's claim to sole representation is tantamount to a potential declaration of War on the DDR,"[10] but that at the same time East Germany was determined to work for an acceptable German and European solution. And in light of declarations such as, "A class struggle aimed at finding an answer to the question 'who dominates whom' has been waged for twenty years between both parts of Germany,"[11] one must indeed wonder if Ulbricht has ever seriously considered the possibility of arriving at a modus vivendi with West Germany through compromise.

6. Kai Hermann, "SED 7th Congress Caught Napping," *Die Zeit*, April 21, 1967; for the English text see *The German Tribune*, No. 264, April 29, 1967, p. 3.
7. "Bonn's innerdeutsche Entspannungspolitik," *Neue Zürcher Zeitung*, April 17, 1967, p. 1.
8. For the text see *Neues Deutschland*, April 18, 1967, pp. 1–2.
9. *Ibid.*, p. 1.
10. *Loc. cit.*
11. *Ibid.*, p. 2.

The Kiesinger-Stoph Letters

In this same strident and confused address, Ulbricht proposed a meeting between the heads of the two German governments in order to "negotiate the first steps toward an intra-German understanding."[12] Such a meeting between Kiesinger and his East German counterpart Willi Stoph never came to pass, but during May and September an exchange of letters took place between them. The Kiesinger-Stoph correspondence confirmed that contacts between the Germanies at that time would resemble a two-sided monologue rather than a dialogue. From the communist side there were only unacceptable demands unaccompanied by anything that would give the slightest hope for reciprocity. In short, the DDR's profound disbelief in the possibility of genuine compromise between the separated parts of Germany was emphatically reconfirmed.

The first letter from East Berlin was sent on May 10 as an answer to Kiesinger's April 12 propositions. Its political substance[13] was nearly identical with that of Ulbricht's New Year's message and the resolutions of the Seventh Party Congress while its main thrust was to emphasize that discussion about "basic political questions"[14] between the two German states was "indispensable"[15] for relaxation of tensions, the letter also contained a thinly-veiled warning that "the obstinate negation of the [present] European situation [which is] the result of the Second World War could only ... [bring] ... damage to the West German population."[16] Finally, it invited Chancellor Kiesinger to conduct negotiations either in East Berlin or in Bonn.

Bonn's new approach to the German question had been just the contrary — to begin exploring the possibility of cooperation in humanitarian and economic matters, without simultaneously trying to reach agreement on far more intractable questions of political principle. Evidently the East German leadership

---

12. *Loc. cit.*
13. For the text of Willi Stoph's letter to Chancellor Kiesinger, see *Neues Deutschland*, No. 129, May 12, 1967, pp. 1–2.
14. *Ibid.*, p. 1.
15. *Loc. cit.*
16. *Ibid.*, p. 2.

hoped that Bonn would be sufficiently eager for further success in its German and Eastern policy to adopt a still more flexible approach at that early date toward the Soviet bloc in general and toward East Germany in particular, even with regard to basic political differences.

The tone of Kiesinger's June 13 response made it clear that the Coalition was determined to keep this channel of communication open, however frustrating it might be.[17] This determination was reaffirmed in subsequent speeches and interviews.[18] Aside from the fact that Kiesinger was obliged indirectly to concede recognition of the Council of Ministers in Berlin when he addressed his letter to its chairman, however, he gave no new ground to the East Germans.

Willi Stoph's second message was delivered on September 18, and it left little room for hope that the DDR was really interested in hammering out a modus vivendi between the two Germanies.[19] In the first letter, the main stumbling block to a normalization of the German affair was said to be the unwillingness of the Federal Republic to cooperate, but the second Stoph letter listed a series of other reasons which also allegedly prevented the two German states from reaching an understanding. The most important among these were Bonn's membership in NATO and in the Common Market, and "the spirit of militarism, and revanchism, as well as the power of monopoly-capitalism"[20] which supposedly informed the thinking of West Germany's business community and political leaders. This list of obstacles was not new. Reiterating them at a time when Bonn was openly searching for formulas which would ease

17. For the text of Chancellor Kiesinger's letter to Willi Stoph, see *Bulletin*, No. 63, June 15, 1967, p. 533.
18. See especially Kiesinger's speech before the *Bundestag* on June 14, "Dem Wohle beider Teile unseres Volkes dienen," *Bulletin*, No. 63, pp. 533–4, and his address on the West German television, "Für menschliche Erleichterungen im geteilten Deutschland," *ibid.*, p. 535. See also his address to the Plenary Session of the *Bundestag* on June 17, "Mit Ernst und Redlichkeit der Freiheit und Einheit unseres Volkes dienen," *Bulletin*, No. 64, June 20, 1967, pp. 541–3. Most indicative of Kiesinger's attitude concerning the letter exchange was his interview with Radio Free Berlin on June 23. For the official text, see *Bulletin*, No. 66, June 23, 1967, pp. 565–6.
19. For the text of Stoph's second letter and for the accompanying draft-treaty, see *Europa Archiv*, Vol. 22, pp. D473–7.
20. *Ibid.*, p. D474.

relations, however, implied that the price for accommodation was for the Federal Republic to sever economic and political ties with the West. This price was of course ridiculously — prohibitively — high. East Germany had in effect ensured rejection of its conditions in advance.

A draft treaty was attached to Stoph's second letter. Its seven articles included the usual East German demands for recognition, sovereign equality, guarantee of existing boundaries, public renunciation of the Munich Agreement, and so forth; there were, on the other hand, no proposals for measures which would preserve the identity of the German nation. The conditions set forth in Stoph's letter and the stipulations of the draft treaty, perhaps inspired in part by the spirit of the Assistance Pacts which had just been signed, suggest that by that time the Ulbricht regime was aiming for much more than de jure recognition by Bonn. From this time on the East Germans acted as though they believed that relentless pressure from them could in fact bring the Federal Republic to completely reorient its entire foreign policy. And if this patently unrealistic goal was not what the Ulbricht regime hoped to gain from the tone of Stoph's second message and the terms of the appended draft treaty — and it is difficult to imagine that it was — then it is not at all clear what in fact they did intend, unless it was to render further serious discussion between the two Germanies impossible.

Herbert Wehner, for one, was nevertheless not wholly discouraged. Most of East Germany's proposals were unacceptable, but there were a few issues, he felt, such as the renunciation of the use of force and economic questions around which, in his opinion, the dialogue could still be continued.[21] Moreover, after several discouraging months of apparent impasse, prospects for other aspects of the Bonn Coalition's new Eastern policy once again seemed to brighten. On August 3, after protracted negotiations, Bonn and Prague agreed to increase

21. See Wehner's interview with the *Parlamentarisch-Politsche Pressedienst*, on September 20, 1967, reprinted in the *Bulletin*, No. 102, September 22, 1967, pp. 876–7. See also Kiesinger's speech in Hamburg on September 19 in which he vigorously advocated the continuation of the Coalition's German policy, reprinted in *ibid.*, pp. 873–5.

trade between their two countries, and even more significantly to exchange permanent official Trade Missions. The agreement was long overdue, and by mid-1967 could hardly have been considered a resounding success for Bonn. But it did demonstrate that for all Ulbricht had raged and lobbied against it, there was still to be a West German political presence in East Europe. And the mere fact that Czechoslovakia had been willing to engage in meaningful political conversations with Bonn exposed the perfunctory nature of the Karlovy Vary resolutions and of the strong language in the recently signed Pact with East Germany. Bonn's position in East Europe was also strengthened by the fact that negotiations[22] which had been begun with Yugoslavia in April finally led to re-establishment of diplomatic relations between the two countries.

West Germany's Reappraisal of its Position

Thus despite the limited success, by the autumn of 1967 it was increasingly apparent that the Great Coalition's new optimistic Eastern policy had ground to a halt. Far from having promoted accommodation between the two Germanies, it had only deepened the rift. The Coalition itself was strained somewhat by differences over how best to pursue its goals in view of these disappointing developments, and it found itself under severe attack from a vocal minority of West German citizens who advocated immediate recognition of the East German regime. Public discussion of the German question thus began anew.

Three important but very different studies appeared in the course of this discussion between September, 1967, and June, 1968. Since each was widely read and commented upon, and since taken together they conveniently define the parameters of the public debate, it will be useful to summarize them briefly here.

The first was a relatively detailed scenario for the evolution of a future Europe on the Gaullist model, published in France

22. Between April 24–29 a German-Yugoslav commission negotiated the extension of the 1964 Trade Agreement along with Yugoslavia's possible cooperation with the GATT.

by the Centre d'Études de Politique Étrangère.[23] In this view Europe could move gradually from *détente* to *entente* and from there to *cooperation* over a period of years. With the help of the former occupying powers relations between the two Germanies would improve as part of the larger context, step by step and stage by stage. Eventually there would be a German Confederation which would preserve much of the political and military identities of each half, but which would unite them in a single parliament of their representatives.

Historical examples of viable confederations — the United States, Switzerland, and the German Federation of 1815–66 — counsel one against automatic skepticism. And the French Plan avoids any pretense of advocating a unitary German state which is in any case an eventuality neither the East nor the West would agree to. Ultimately, however, the French study raises more questions than it can answer. It deals inadequately in particular with the central problem of how a viable German confederation capable of serving as the linch-pin of a politically stable Europe *can* be created between two political entities with such heterogenous social and political structure, unremittingly hostile ideologies and diametrically opposed foreign policy preferences. Only by ignoring the weight of these vexed questions could the French study have come to the remarkably optimistic conclusions it did.

The second important study outlining possible solutions to the German question was published in March, 1968, by the Evangelical Church.[24] The document was by no means universally endorsed by the Church itself. Nevertheless the document contains some noteworthy aspects. In this view a politically stable European arrangement would include the presence of the two superpowers, but "the independent nation states . . . without responsibility to supranational institutions is

23. Un group de recherches, "Model de sécurité éuropéene," *Centre d'études de Politique Étrangère*, Vol. 32, No. 6 (September, 1967), pp. 519–41.
24. *Friedensaufgaben der Deutschen*, Kammer der Evangelischen Kirche in Deutschland für öffentliche Verantwortung, March 1, 1968, reprinted in *Europa Archiv*, Vol. 23, No. 12, June 25, 1968, pp. D273–82. Cf. another study initiated by the Bensberger Kreis, entitled *Memorandum deutscher Katholiken zu den polnisch-deutschen Fragen* (Grünewald Verlag, Mainz, 1968).

[considered to be] once and for all obsolete."[25] If this is the Europe for which to work, the study then asks "In what way could the Germans contribute to the guarantee of peace?" and "Is peace best guaranteed if Germany remains divided?"[26] This study like the French one before it envisaged eventual confederation rather than outright reunification of the two Germanies, but within a non-Gaullist general context. The permanent character of the communist socio-political order in East Germany was tacitly accepted. While it failed to come to grips with the stubborn problems created by the nature of communist ideology, the EKD study remains one of the most valuable contributions to the search for a solution of the German question. To quote one of the most realistic German observers of foreign affairs, "it was the first time that a concept was developed among people from both parts of Germany . . . without tactical finesses and propaganda cliches and . . . without slandering the other's system."[27]

The third of the three studies, a memorandum by Wolfgang Schütz, stirred particularly animated debate within West Germany.[28] Schütz asserted that a pan-German community could be negotiated gradually through a series of agreements which would not touch at all on the sensitive questions of de jure and de facto recognition. The governing principle of this process was to be mutual acceptance of the fact that the German nation itself had remained indivisible, regardless of the fact that its members were presently living under entirely different social, and political systems. Recognition as such was thus beside the point. Neither the principle, nor the process stood any serious chances of being endorsed by East Germany, but the fact that the widely circulated Schütz proposals went beyond official West German policy in searching for ways to move toward accommodation was itself a valuable contribution.

25. "Friedensaufgaben . . . ," *op. cit.*, p. D276.
26. *Ibid.*, p. D278.
27. Marion Gräfin Dönhoff, "Ein Konzept für Deutschland," *Die Zeit*, March 12, 1968, p. 3.
28. Wilhelm Wolfgang Schütz, "Was ist Deutschland? Denkmodelle für eine deutsche Gemeinschaft," *Kuratorium Unteilbares Deutschland* (Berlin, 1968). The memorandum was much discussed in Germany, and most of the comments were summarized in *Deutschland-Memorandum: Eine Denkschrift und ihre Folgen* (Fischer Bücherei, Frankfurt/Main, 1968) (pamphlet).

Deepening the Cleavage

In the same period during which these three studies and others appeared in the West discussing strategies and principles which would provide a basis for eventual reconciliation between the two halves of Germany, East Germany for its part published two documents that could only deepen the cleavage: the new Constitution, and the new Penal Code.

East Germany's first constitution had been adopted in 1949. It bore traces of the liberal democratic concepts which had guided the Weimar Republic, and it neither denied the possibility nor the desirability of a reunited Germany. The Constitution promulgated in early 1968, by contrast, is devoid of legal or historical continuity since it is built entirely around political concepts associated with Soviet Marxism. The passages dealing with the legal and moral status of the two Germanies are hardly conducive to rapprochement on any level.

The Preamble to the new Constitution declares that the future not only of East Germany but of the whole German nation will be one characterized by "peace and socialism." These happy conditions have been denied the German people to date by "the forces of imperialism and capitalism" which have split the nation. Since peace is to be achieved only through socialism, it follows that the East German state — by dint of its social and political structure — is in effect the sole true representative of the interests of the German people.

Article 8 is more explicit. Cooperation with Bonn can be carried on only within a framework of "normal interstate relations" based on sovereign equality. The division of the German nation can be ended only "on the basis of socialism and democracy." In effect then the main pre-condition set forth for the German nation's reunification whatever its form is the imposition of the DDR's social, political and economic structure on West German society. The new Constitution is thus completely congruent with Ulbricht's January, 1968, declaration that the German question is only a peculiar instance of the class struggle, and contacts between East and West Germany should be approached with that in mind.[29]

29. Ulbricht's intentions in this respect were revealed in his January 31

The DDR's intention of making a break with the pan-German past was even more evident in the new Penal Code promulgated in January, 1968. The old Penal Code of 1871, amended so many times since 1949 that by the mid-1960's it served only as a nominal basis for East German jurisprudence, was formally annulled. While it is understandable that the East German government would want to codify and clarify the legal system, as a political act the new Penal Code went far beyond a mere formal summation of principles and practices which had been in effect for many years.

In 1967 there had been legislation regulating citizenship in the DDR.[30] According to this law every German citizen who lived on East German territory in 1949 would be considered subject to the DDR's jursidiction in perpetuity. Article 99 of the new Penal Code defines "treasonable disloyalty" to the state as a criminal act punishable by death, which can specifically include the behavior of individuals living outside the DDR who engaged in "activities hostile to the state." It is obvious that in practice such elastic stipulations could be used indiscriminately against virtually any East German refugee.

The new Penal Code goes beyond even this questionable claim to jurisdiction over former citizens. Article 106 includes "discriminatory criticism" of the DDR's social and political order, of its organs, representatives and other citizens if such criticism is expressed through publications or organs engaged in a struggle against the East German regime under the rubric "agitation hostile to the state." West German and even non-German journalists, scholars and others could be prosecuted under this Article as it is written. Moreover, it is perfectly possible that the East Germans might apply this section of their Penal Code to West German governmental officials. Nor are West German or non-German businessmen likely to fare better. Article 103 sets the penalty for "economic subversion" at from

---

speech before the East Berlin *Volkskammer* when he said that "the question of the [German] nation is only a class-problem which can be solved only by eliminating imperialism, monopol-capitalism and neo-nazism in the Federal Republic," *Neues Deutschland*, February 1, 1968, pp. 1–2.
30. *Gesetz über die Staatsbürgerschaft der Deutschen Demokratischen Republik*, given in excerpt in *Neues Deutschland*, No. 52, February 21, 1967.

two to fifteen years' imprisonment, and extremely "aggravated cases" may be punishable by death. These draconian sections of the new Penal Code stand in sharp contrast to the extraordinarily permissive sections that deal with non-political crimes such as perjury, theft, robbery, murder, divorce, bigamy, homosexuality and sexual crimes.

One is forced to conclude that the East German's new criminal law has a dual objective. On the one hand in exercising permissiveness toward non-political crimes and offenses it aims at weakening and eventually destroying the old value basis of the East German society, thus accelerating the pace of differentiating it from West Germany. If this assumption is correct, one could say that in this respect the Penal Code could be more dangerous for the future of the German nation than the extremely harsh penalties for political crimes which aim basically at the defense of a system, the future of which after all has not been adequately secured. Consequently, the new Penal Code along with the Constitution must be regarded as a typically aggressive instrument of Ulbricht's class struggle directed against Bonn and against every attempt at an intra-German reconciliation.

Ulbricht's uncompromising public stands, the fruitless Kiesinger-Stoph correspondence and, finally, the pointed intransigence conveyed in the new Constitution and the new Penal Code caused relations between East and West Germany to plummet toward the freezing point by the spring of 1968. Bonn's every move toward conciliation had been countered at every turn, as a few skeptics had predicted, by less and less flexibility from the Ulbricht regime. The Great Coalition's new Eastern policy may or may not have offered compromises sufficient to have served as a basis for negotiating the terms of gradual relaxation: the point is that they were never given a serious chance. To understand fully why West Germany's initiative met the fate it did, however, it is necessary to move back to discussion of the dramatic and unexpected changes which were taking place even then in the rest of East Europe.

7

the
czechoslovak crisis

Declining Soviet Influence

Zbigniew Brzezinski in his classic study on the Soviet bloc lists five "immediate objectives" which determined the Soviet Union's policy toward Eastern Europe during and after World War II.[1] These objectives are (1) to exert Soviet influence in Eastern Europe in order to deny this area to Germany; (2) the sovietization of Eastern Europe in order to provide the USSR with a *cordon sanitaire* between the USSR and Germany; (3) to use the area for purposes of Soviet economic recovery; (4) to deny the area to the capitalist world; and (5) to use it as a base for further Soviet expansion. For the purposes of the present study the first and second of these objectives deserve special attention, because they not only affected the Soviet pattern of behavior toward Eastern Europe but also determined the Kremlin's long-range policy toward Germany. After the traumatic experiences of the Second World War, the first requirement for the security of the Soviet Union was to establish its influence in Eastern Europe in order "to deny the area to

1. Zbigniew Brzezinski, *The Soviet Bloc, Unity and Conflict* (revised edition) (Frederick A. Praeger, New York, 1967), pp. 4–5.

Germany."[2] However, in the long run the mere establishment of a Soviet-style *cordon sanitaire* on its Western perimeter would have been inadequate had the permanency of the Soviet Union's political and military presence in Eastern Europe not been secured. Hence, the second basic objective, the sovietization of Eastern Europe, was intended to make the existing regimes politically, economically, and militarily dependent on the Kremlin. The USSR has apparently never deviated from these objectives. Ever since 1945 Soviet foreign policy has sought to make Eastern Europe immune to any kind of German penetration, and to secure Soviet political, military, economic and ideological predominance in this area against challenges from without as well as from within.

To be sure, the Soviet Union has never succeeded in achieving complete ideological and/or institutional uniformity in Eastern Europe, a condition which Stalin considered essential for the Kremlin's predominance. The Yugoslav heresy of 1948 along with the Polish and Hungarian attempts at national emancipation in 1956 seriously weakened, even if only temporarily, the Soviet influence in Eastern Europe. However, in spite of ideological diversity, reflected in different and often contradictory approaches toward achieving socialism, a certain degree of cohesion has existed within the Soviet bloc. The emergence of anti-Russian sentiments, the presence of anti-colonialism directed against the Soviet Union, and the desire to reassert national identity have at times represented a serious threat to Soviet predominance in Eastern Europe. Furthermore, ideological de-stalinization has been followed by theoretical and practical changes in the economic field. For some time these forces have been present and active, if only below the surface in Eastern Europe. In the case of Rumania, they have even been politically articulated. Yet to the extent that these forces and factors have been kept under control, the relative inner cohesion of Eastern Europe under Soviet hegemony has remained secure. This fact in turn ensured a relatively uniform foreign policy pattern toward the West in general and toward the German question in particular.

2. *Loc. cit.*

Lest the above statements be misinterpreted, one must emphasize that ever since the early 1960's the "unity" of the East European Communist bloc has been eroding. In many cases the uniformity in foreign policy platforms has been maintained more by Soviet pressure than by local political conviction. However, it was not until 1968 that common foreign policy and Soviet predominance in Eastern Europe came under serious attacks. The erosion of communist unity became clearly visible at the Consultative Conference held in Budapest[3] in February, 1968.

The Budapest Conference

The alleged purpose of the Budapest meeting was to lay the basis for a world communist conference later in the year. However, the Consultative Conference, which was followed by a series of further consultations during the summer, had two further objectives: first, to establish, or better to re-establish, ideological unity among the Communist Parties, and second, on this basis to create a united front against "imperialism." Needless to say, the acceptance of both objectives would have meant tacit acceptance of Soviet leadership in ideological and foreign policy matters. The Parties assembled in the Danubian capital did ultimately agree in principle on the necessity to convoke a World Communist Conference in Moscow later in the year, presumably with the purpose of condemning Red China for ideological heresy. There was even agreement on an increased struggle against "imperialism." However, consensus on ideological unity was not obtained nor was Moscow's leadership re-established.

The fact that six of the ruling Communist Parties were either not invited (Yugoslavia) or did not accept the invitation (Albania, Cuba, North Korea, North Vietnam and Red China) and that only 64 Communist Parties were represented at the Conference was ample evidence of the prevailing com-

3. For an excellent short discussion of Communist unity see Canfield F. Smith, "The Rocky Road to Unity," *East Europe*, Vol. 18, No. 2 (February, 1969), pp. 3-10; for remarks on the Budapest Conference, see especially pp. 4 ff.

munist disunity. Even more important was Moscow's inability (due to the reluctance of those present) to forge an outwardly monolithic unit out of a Commonwealth which during the last few years has become increasingly pluralistic in spite of its adherence to communist theory and practice. In order to understand Moscow's actions later in the year and the Soviet introduction of the idea of "limited sovereignty" as a governing principle of intra-communist relations, it is imperative to note that the real issue at Budapest was whether or not loyalty to "international solidarity" would prevail over the requirements of national communism. This basic contradiction was recognized prior to the Conference by the East European mass media, most notably by the Hungarian newspapers.[4] While all of them emphasized that the main goal of the Conference was to establish "anti-imperialist unity of action," they also pointed out that within its own national domain every Communist Party should possess complete freedom of action and decision. As to how this contradiction could be solved there was no answer in the Hungarian press. The official organ of the Hungarian Party stated that "the Communist parties have equal responsibility toward the national as well as toward the international requirements of the Communist movement."[5] At the same time the spokesman of the Labor Union maintained that "the unity among the [Communist] Parties cannot be brought about by outside pressure, but only through a mutual agreement on common interests arrived at in a free and uninhibited discussion."[6]

The reluctance to submit to Moscow's leadership was most clearly expressed at the Conference by the Italian and Rumanian delegates, the former demanding the establishment of a genuine "popular front" against imperialism which should include non-communist but leftist parties, and the latter rejecting in toto the idea of revitalizing the Cominform or Comintern in any form. Twenty or even fifteen years earlier the

4. See the editorials in *Népszava*, and *Magyar Nemzet*, February 25, 1968, p. 1.
5. "Questions to be Solved," editorial in *Népszabadság*, February 24, 1968, p. 1.
6. "The Equality of the Socialist States," editorial in *Népszava*, February 26, 1968, p. 1.

Kremlin would have reacted to such open heresy with its customary ruthlessness. But in 1968 in order to bridge the unbridgeable, it had to resort to more subtle means. To this effect Moscow selected as its spokesman (aside from Suslov) the Chief Secretary of the Hungarian Communist Party, János Kádár, who did his best to achieve the Soviet objectives. However, he failed to harmonize the centristic tendencies of the Soviet Union with the increasing desire of the indigenous Communist Parties for more independence. Even Kádár noted that "the last years' serious theoretical, philosophical and political differences of opinions within the Socialist camp have become so deep"[7] as to endanger its cohesion. Moreover, he could not convince his audience that "a united front does not necessarily imply even the partial loss of independence."[8] It is imperative to realize that in 1968 "imperialism" no longer had the same connotation to the East European Communists as it had to the Soviet Union. Nor were the East Europeans willing to accept the notion that "imperialism" and the United States (and its chief Western ally, Germany) were synonymous. It must have sounded highly ironic to some of the delegates in Budapest when Kádár accused the United States and other "imperialists" of "trampling the most elementary requirements of international law, of applying political and economic pressure to sovereign states, and of initiating armed conflicts in various parts of the world."[9]

The highlight of the Budapest Conference came when the Rumanian delegation walked out on the third day.[10] The Rumanian walk-out was more than a simple affront to the Soviet Union. On the one hand, it demonstrated the growing

---

7. Secretary Kádár's speech reprinted in excerpts in *Népszabadság*, February 27, 1968, pp. 1–2; see also "Kádár Condemns U.S. Imperialism," *The New York Times*, February 27, 1968.
8. *Ibid.*, p. 2.
9. *Loc. cit.*
10. Subsequent to this event the Rumanian Communists issued an exceedingly sharp-worded resolution which is indicative of Rumania's concept of "socialist international solidarity," and clearly reflects the degree of independence the Party has sought. For this, see "Resolution of the Central Committee of the Rumanian Communist Party on the Consultative Conference in Budapest," *Agerpress*, "Documents, Articles, and Information on Rumania," No. 6, *Supplement*, March 2, 1969, pp. 1–5.

discrepancy between the Soviet Union's increasing military power (in both the absolute and relative sense of the word) and its steadily declining political influence in Eastern Europe. On the other hand, Rumania's unilateral action indicated Moscow's temporary inability to restrain the visible trend toward an increasing ideological schism within the communist movement. The Soviet Union even seems to have encouraged these tendencies by declaring the "impermissibility of . . . excommunication by one single center."[11] Yet, was it not erroneous to equate Rumania's insubordination with the Soviet-Yugoslav rupture of 1948? Was it not premature to prophesy the inevitable disintegration of Moscow's political and ideological influence in Eastern Europe?[12] Finally, was it not exaggerated to hope that Rumania's temporary and very limited secession from the Soviet bloc would hasten the process of European reconciliation?

In 1968 the answer to all such questions would have been affirmative. It was true that Rumania was permitted to leave the Conference unpunished. In contrast to Tito's expulsion in 1948, the excommunication of Rumania was not even attempted. It was also true that in Budapest Moscow encountered serious difficulties in pressuring its now reluctant client states to accept a common foreign policy. Furthermore, no one could have missed the evidence of Moscow's declining appeal at the Conference where many speakers presented opinions divergent from those of Moscow. But it was equally true that two very important considerations came to the forefront which will long remain the basic determinants of Soviet-East European relations: first, that in the shadow of the Soviet Union's formidable military power the foregin policy aspirations of the peripheral national-communist states will always occupy a second place;

11. See especially Suslov's speech in Budapest, reprinted in *Neues Deutschland*, February 29, pp. 1–3, and in excerpts in *Népszabadság*, February 29, p. 1. See also the *Communiqué* issued at the end of the Budapest meeting placing great emphasis on the independence of the Communist Parties, reprinted in *Neues Deutschland*, March 6, 1968, pp. 1–3.
12. Harry Hamm, "The Rumanians Bravely Pursue an Independent Line," *Frankfurter Allgemeine Zeitung*, March 4, 1968, reprinted in *The German Tribune*, No. 309, March 16, 1968, pp. 1–3; see also "Abgang und Zuwachs der sowjetischen Buchhaltung," *Neue Zürcher Zeitung*, March 3, 1968, p. 1.

second, that the issue of ideological purity and disciplinary measures against heresy will always be subordinated to the requirements of Soviet Union's foreign policy as a great power.

It is true that in 1956, after the traumatic years of Stalinism, Eastern Europe experienced its first political spring, and out of the Polish and tragic Hungarian attempts at a forceful exploration of the limits of freedom, there emerged a certain "model for emancipation." It was based on the assumption that relative domestic political freedom can and *must* be bought at the price of absolute conformity with the objectives of Soviet foreign policy. Gomulka's "voluntary" assurance completely to subordinate Poland's foreign policy to the interests of the Kremlin bought him permission to steer his country toward national communism. On the other hand, Hungary's attempt to shake off the fetters of the Warsaw Pact resulted in an immediate armed intervention. To be sure, the model did not remain unchanged. Rumania was able to emancipate itself from Soviet economic tutelage partly by skillfully exploiting the Sino-Soviet dispute, partly by relying on its abundance of industrial raw materials. Hungary was permitted to experiment with an unprecedented amount of domestic liberalization. However, in reality none of these developments, not even Rumania's insubordination in Budapest, indicate an end to Soviet influence and control in Eastern Europe. On the contrary, in practice the limits of Soviet tolerance have since been clearly defined. There undoubtedly has existed a certain degree of permissiveness on the Kremlin's part toward limited economic independence wherever the conditions were favorable to such experiment, but only as long as the process did not jeopardize the primary power and security interests of the Soviet Union. Within the same limits, it has also been possible to carry out domestic political reforms, even if, as in Hungary's case, they involved some moderate ideological deviations. In Budapest it was apparent that the majority of the East European Communists were more interested in obtaining as much political and economic independence as the narrow limits of communist collectivity permitted than in assisting Moscow in its endeavors to create a united front against imperialism. But since Budapest it also became apparent that while the Soviet

Union might permit such unorthodox practices, it would quickly reassert control when it felt its vital interests threatened.

Background of the Czech Crisis

Nowhere were the limits of Soviet tolerance and its determination to maintain the status quo better demonstrated than in the brutal suppression of Czechoslovakia's attempt at national and ideological emancipation. Moreover, nothing illustrated better the bankruptcy of the old communist system to the communist societies themselves than its temporary disintegration in Prague during January and February, 1968. Finally, nothing unveiled more dramatically the real Soviet concepts of a European *détente* and a European security arrangement than the stationing of Red Army units along the Western boundaries of Czechoslovakia. The events in that country (which one commentator called a "euphoric revolution," and another the "Spring between two Winters")[13] were much more than a promise to transform community totalitarianism into socialist democracy. They could have heralded the beginning of the long overdue inter-European reconciliation had they been permitted to reach their logical conclusion.

It will not be necessary here to follow the exact chronology of these events which began in the Summer of 1967 and came to an abrupt end on August 21, 1968. They have been analyzed by a variety of competent sources.[14] However, it is important

13. Anatole Shub, "Prague: Euphoria of Revolution," *The Washington Post*, March 15, 1968, p. A10, and Tad Szulc, "A Spring of Freedom is Cut Short in Czechoslovakia," *The New York Times*, September 1, 1968, p. E3.

14. The best brief analysis of the Czechoslovakian events is contained in Ivan Svitak, "Before the Occupation: The Political Crisis in Czechoslovakia," *East Europe*, Vol. 17, No. 10 (October, 1968), pp. 13–16, and in James H. Billington's already quoted article in *Foreign Affairs*, Billington, "Forces and Factors," *op cit.*, *passim*. See also Josef Krucky, "Upsurge in Czechoslovakia," *East Europe*, Vol. 17, No. 9 (September, 1968), p. 307; also Christopher Bryant, "Prague Summer: 1968," *ibid.*, pp. 7-10. An account of the first phase of the political development in Czechoslovakia can be found in Andreas Razumovsky, "Die Wachablösung," *Osteuropa*, Vol. 18, No. 3 (March, 1968), pp. 161–75, cf. Hans Lemberg, "Die Intervention in Prag: Stationen, Ursachen — Ein erstes Fazit," *Osteuropa*, Vol. 18, No. 10/11 (October/November, 1968), pp. 697–708. For more detailed accounts see Philip Windsor and Adam Roberts, *Czechoslovakia 1968, Reform, Repression*

to place in proper perspective the forces and factors which precipitated the crisis, and to analyze the impact of the crisis on the further development of Soviet-East European relations. Finally, attention must be focused on the effect of the crisis on Soviet policy toward Western Europe in general and toward West Germany in particular.

It is a political truism that revolutions do not appear overnight. Nor do uprisings against a colonizing power come about suddenly. Revolutions and anti-colonial uprisings are usually the end-results of a long, drawn-out process during which various factors and forces interact. However, even if all the pre-conditions are present, drastic structural and ideological changes cannot be politically articulated without intellectual preparation. The latter crystallizes the prevalent dissent, dissatisfaction and expectations for the future of the society. It provides the necessary ideological impetus, and ultimately marks the direction of change. Only after this process has run its full circle does the situation ensue in which — to paraphrase Lenin — the society develops an irreconcilable antagonism toward the existing social, political and economic order.

In the mid-1960's all the preconditions for a drastic but not necessarily violent change were present in Czechoslovakia. There was a longstanding dissatisfaction with the country's economic conditions. There was dissent from communist ideology, which had lost its adequacy as the compulsory guideline for an increasingly pluralistic industrial society. There was the accumulation of a profound hatred against the arbitrary power of the State and the Party. Finally there was the latent expectation of a change which could bring about a politically less oppressive, economically more efficient and ideologically non-doctrinaire order in which the individual could freely reassert his identity.

Probably the most important of the long-term factors which precipitated the crisis was the country's economic malaise, which culminated in the years 1963–4. From this time on we can discern a curious development in Czechoslovakia. On the

---

and Resistance (Columbia University Press, New York, 1969), Robert Littel (ed.), *The Czech Black Book*, Prepared by the Institute of History of the Czechoslovak Academy of Sciences (Frederick A. Praeger, New York, 1969) and Z. A. B. Zeman, *Prague Spring* (Hill and Wang, New York, 1969).

one hand the 13th Party Congress by the Party in 1966 pledged itself to become the avant-garde in carrying out economic reforms.[15] On the other hand, by 1967 there was the increasing realization that the "greatest threat to Czechoslovakia's economic recovery is an indiscriminate spirit of compromise, which makes too many allowances for past mistakes and tries to soften the effects of change."[16] Moreover, in 1967 it was realized (especially by Professor Ota Sik and his followers) that the economic plight of the country could be remedied only if the central planning were minimized and maximum emphasis placed on entrepreneurial freedom and on production efficiency.

However, it was obvious that the rigorous application of such unorthodox measures, which aimed at nothing less than the transformation of a centrally planned economy into a market oriented one, would encounter considerable initial difficulties. It was to be expected that the proposed rationalization of the Czechoslovakian economy would evoke the reluctance of the workers themselves, who would inevitably be faced either with reduced income or in the worst case with unemployment. Furthermore, rationalization would have increased the already vocal dissent of those bureaucrats and "aparatchiki" who saw in the economic reforms a mortal threat to their vested interests.[17] In 1967 it was obvious that in order to carry out such initially unpopular reforms more courage and practical imagination was required than the Party functionaries under the leadership of Novotny had ever possessed, They could not or would not envisage the beneficial effects of the proposed reforms beyond the initial difficulties. Nevertheless, by the end of 1967 the majority of the Central Committee became more or

15. For an excellent discussion of Czechoslovakia's economic plight and of the planned remedies, see Radoslav Selucki, *Reformmodell USSR, Entwurf einer Socialistischen Marktwirtschaft* (Rowohlt Verlag, Hamburg, 1969); and Vaclav Holesovsky, "Prague's Economic Model," *East Europe*, Vol. 16, No. 2 (February, 1967), pp. 13–17.
16. Jiri Kanturek, "Reform: Full Victory or Hesitant Steps," *Kulturni Tvorba*, January 5, 1967, pp. 6–7. For the reluctance of certain factions within the Party toward economic reforms, see Jan F. Triska, "The Party Aparatchik at Bay," *East Europe*, Vol. 16, No. 12 (December, 1967), pp. 2–8.
17. Triska, *op. cit.*, p. 4.

less converted to the idea of the new economic experiment.[18]

Simultaneously with this challenge to the Party's ability and preparedness in economic matters, its political, intellectual and moral leadership also came under serious attack, this time from the quarter of communist writers and other intellectuals within the Party. By 1967 the truce which had been worked out in 1963 and which enabled the Czechoslovakian writers "to shake off their Stalinist fetters at a remarkable speed"[19] came to an abrupt end at the Fourth Congress of the Writer's Union.[20]

At the Congress, which was not lacking in turbulent scenes, the most important speakers[21] went much beyond a mere criticism of the Party's role in intellectual matters. They condemned the Party for the devastating results of its twenty years' cultural monopoly, and for the country's cultural and political absence from Europe. They indicted the Party for the abuse of its power which had dehumanized the individual, and which was responsible for the unprecedented low level of morals and ethics in the country. Finally, the Congress, through its spokesmen, expressed its deep concern that there were no political guarantees against the arbitrary use of power by the Party.

However, the speeches, which in their straightforwardness surpassed even Djilas' *New Class*, also pleaded indirectly for democratization, for a redistribution of power between Party and State, and for the reinstatement of the individual to his rightful position in society. Moreover, the spirit of the Congress

18. See L. E. Knight, "Czechoslovakia's Fading Old Guard," *East Europe*, Vol. 16, No. 11 (November, 1967), pp. 15–18.
19. For an exceptionally good analytical description of the Conference see Rudolf Urban, "Der verwegene Geist; der IV. Kongress tschechoslovakischer Schriftsteller und seine Folgen," *Osteuropa*, Vol. 18, No. 3 (March, 1968), pp. 176–99.
20. *Ibid.*, p. 176.
21. The most important speech was delivered by Ludvik Vaculik. Charac-teristically, none of the Czechoslovakian newspapers published his speech. The *Literarni Noviny*, No. 27, July 8, 1967, published only its title, "The Relationship Between Citizen and Power, Between Power and Culture." Excerpts of the speech appeared only later in Switzerland and West Germany. See "Power and Resistance," *Die Weltwoche*, July 21, 1967, pp. 1–2, and *Frankfurter Allgemeine Zeitung*, July 24, 1967, p. 1. For the full text (in German) which was broadcasted by *Radio Free Europe* on August 22, 23 and 24, see "Rede des tschechischen Schriftstellers Ludvik Vaculik an dem IV. Kongress tschechoslovakischer Schriftsteller," *Osteuropa*, Vol. 18, No. 3 (March, 1968), pp. 233–43.

actually expressed the prevailing sentiments of the majority of the population. In this respect it can be equated with the 1956 Petöfi Club in Hungary, which was most instrumental in precipitating the dismissal of the Stalinist regime. Never before in Hungary, not even during the pre-revolutionary period, had the Party's inhuman character, its corruptive power, and its alienation from the ruled been exposed by communists themselves to such an extent as in that summer in Czechoslovakia.

Yet the Party's reaction to this fierce attack was hesitant. Although it expelled several of the writers from its ranks, and although it placed the Writers Union journal under strict governmental control, both the Party and the State refrained from further prosecuting the dissidents. The only plausible explanation for this leniency is that by this time the reform-minded elements in the Party had become a majority which realized that the latter's political survival depended not only on economic liberalization but also on a speedy democratization of the entire political structure. Thus it seems safe to say that by the end of the year the Party was ripe for a "revolution from above," an unheard of occurrence in the annals of communist history.

In addition to the economists and intellectuals within the Party there existed another group which, according to one source,[22] consisted mostly of political scientists and experts in international affairs, and which registered increasing dissatisfaction with both domestic and foreign affairs. Moreover, by this time even the highest echelons of the Party came to realize the absolute necessity of reforms. On Novotny's initiative an interdepartmental research team was assigned the task of solving questions concerning the development of the political system and of democracy in socialist society.[23] According to various sources the result of this research was the advocacy of the introduction of a moderately pluralistic political model, presumably along Yugoslav lines, in the country's political structure.[24]

22. See Deryck E. Viney, "Der Demokratisierungsprozess in der Tschecho-slovakei", *Europa Archiv*, Vol. 23, No. 12 (June 25, 1968), pp. 423–38.
23. "Some Questions for Political Scientists," *Rude Pravo*, July 26, 1967.
24. Viney, *op. cit.*, p. 425; see also Zdenek Mylnar's interview with *Rude*

Much of this ferment developed within the Party itself. However, the disillusionment within the Party and the resolve of the majority of its leadership to introduce liberal economic and political measures were the clearly reflected expectations of the society itself. On the other hand, it would be a great error to maintain that the Party embodied *all* sentiments which were prevalent in Czechoslovakia. It certainly did not become the spokesman of the post-ideological generation,[25] nor did it associate itself at this time with the emerging nationalistic tendencies of the population. Yet both these forces were highly instrumental in precipitating the change of the guard in the Hradcany Palace. Moreover, most of the forces and ideas which contributed to the emergence of the new Party leadership were clearly reflected in the new government's program. Herein lies the unique character of the Czechoslovakian events, because by associating itself, at least in the beginning, with the overwhelming majority of popular sentiment the Party was able to channel most of the political dissatisfaction and economic expectations in such a way that a peaceful transition from Stalinism to a more liberal but still communist course might have taken place.

The April Action Program

In January, Antonin Novotny, the man most identified with the repressions of the 1950's and the failures of the 1960's, was replaced as the Secretary General of the Party by Alexander Dubcek. Far reaching changes took place both in the Party and in the governmental personnel, and by the end of February the new leadership embarked on a reform program, some of whose guidelines appear in the party's Action Program published in April, 1968.[26]

Pravo on February 13, 1968, excerpts of which were reprinted in *East Europe*, Vol. 17, No. 4 (April, 1968), pp. 33–35.
25. In his frequently quoted article Billington describes the youth in East Europe with this term. The author who in 1968 had ample opportunity to talk to a representative cross section of the young generation (mostly university students) wishes to add that the postwar generation is definitely anti-ideological regardless of whether it is Communist or Western ideology. The same applies to matters of religion.
26. *The Action Program of the Czechoslovak Communist Party*, CTK, April, 1968,

The Action Program covered domestic political liberalization, the drive for economic liberalization, and most interesting
for our purposes, the reformulation of foreign policy. The
Program advanced some very unorthodox propositions in the
field of foreign trade;[27] its main objective in this area was to
guide the country's economy back into the mainstream of international competition from which it had been isolated for
many years. Individual enterprises were to be more independent in their choice of exports and imports, and these and other
measures were to lead ultimately to the convertibility of the
Czechoslovak currency. A new and more realistic investment
price policy would erase the discrepancy between domestic and
world prices. The new leadership assured the Socialist Camp
that "continuous economic cooperation with other socialist
countries, especially with members of COMECON will remain
the basis of our international relations."[28] But as if to emphasize
the inadequacy of these ties alone for Czechoslovakia's effective
economic recovery, the Program immediately thereafter proposed increased economic cooperation with all other nations of
the world. The Party further pledged its support to an intensified exchange of technological know-how, presumably with the
West, and advocated a policy which would attract foreign
credits and capital investment.

The final part of the Program dealt directly with foreign
policy per se. Although some commentators have described
these passages as cursory[29] one does not have to know how to
read in between the lines of a communist document in order to
discover that this part of the Program represented a reorientation of Czech foreign policy. Brief as it is, the April Program
left little doubt that important changes in Czechoslovakia's
foreign policy were in the offing. Czechoslovakia would honor
its treaty obligations and continue to cooperate closely with the
Soviet Union and other socialist states. But Czechoslovakia's

---

reprinted in excerpts in *Europa Archiv*, Vol. 23, No. 13 (July, 1968), pp.
D289–304. See also *Governmental Declaration of Prime Minister Oldrich Cernik on
April 24, 1968*, Czechoslovak Digest, No. 18/19, April, 1968.
27. *The Action Program . . .* , *op. cit.*, pp. D301 ff.
28. *Ibid.*, p. D302.
29. Derick E. Viney, *op. cit.*, p. 424.

relative passivity in foreign affairs was deplored: "We did neither exhaust every possibility . . . nor did our foreign policy possess independent initiatives concerning a series of international problems."[30] The Program urged the Central Committee, the Foreign Ministry and the Parliament to "correct this short-coming so that our foreign policy will completely correspond to the requirements of the national interest of socialist Czecho-slovakia."[31] "Our geographic position, along with the needs of an industrialized society," the Action Program continues, "demands a more active European policy."[32]

If one agrees with Kurt London's axiom that "the most in-genious policy is no better than its application,"[33] it is safe to say that the policy of liberalization in Czechoslovakia contained the germs of its own destruction. To be sure the policy was re-sourceful and under other conditions it could have been success-fully implemented. Some commentators said that the reforms were "too little and too late."[34] On the contrary, it was a program which proposed too much and too suddenly without adequate safeguards to regulate the transition from totalitarian-ism to a more moderate form of communism.

Political upheavals are akin to wars, for they also develop their own laws and generate their own dynamism. Can a Communist Party, liberal as it may be, preserve its leading role in state and society if it is daily exposed to the challenges of free criticism, press, and discussion? In Czechoslovakia the definite erosion of the Party's political power became soon apparent, in spite of the leadership's determination to preserve the Party as the leading political force in the country. Furthermore, the abolition of censorship, the almost unrestricted freedom of the mass media, and the freedom to criticize heralded the emer-gence of a genuine opposition. Had such opposition material-

30. *The Action Program . . .* , *op. cit.*, p. 431.
31. *Ibid.*, p. D303.
32. *Ibid.*, p. D304.
33. Kurt London, *The Permanent Crisis* (2nd ed.) (Blaisdell Publishing Company, Waltham, Massachusetts, 1968).
34. Richard Eder, "Czech Discount Scope of Reform," *The New York Times*, April 11, 1968, quoting Professor Svitak who said that "democratiza-tion never is and never has been the political objective of the new set fighting for power," See also "Freiheitsfieber in Prag und Warschau," *Neue Zürcher Zeitung*, March 17, 1968, pp. 1–2.

ized the new leadership would have been left with two alternatives. The first option would have been to subscribe to the rules of the democratic process and thus to accept the fact that the Party could not realistically aspire even to the position of *primus inter pares*. The second alternative would have meant the resort to the old methods in an attempt to restore the Party to its leading position. In both cases the days of the Party's political life would have been numbered.

Yet even if by some miracle the Party succeeded in presenting itself as a genuine democratic force, it is doubtful how much longer it could have withstood the pressure of increasing demands for more democratization and the desire for a more accentuated national identity. In 1968 the Czechoslovakian people suddenly remembered their successful experience with democracy, and as national symbols Masaryk and Benes were infinitely more important to the majority of the population than Lenin.

Moreover, could Dubcek and his fellow Liberals promise that the germ of freedom would remain within the confines of Czechoslovakia? It should be emphasized that the political upheaval in Czechoslovakia was not an isolated occurrence. The Polish student revolts, the sympathetic attitudes of Yugoslavia and Rumania, and the covert enthusiasm of Hungarian public opinion toward the reforms in Prague were all expressions of those latent forces in East Europe which were about to be politically articulated in Czechoslovakia. The lifting of censorship and the not-so-tentative moves toward democratizing political life in Czechoslovakia posed a great threat to the conservative leaders of the Soviet bloc. Not only were such heady reforms certain to prove contagious, but there was no guarantee that in the long run the reformers in the Czechoslovakian Communist Party themselves would be able to control the forces they had unleashed. If Czechoslovakia evolved along the lines of a very leftist but nevertheless Western type of social democracy, even the Soviet system, not to mention those of its far less stable East European fiefs, might have found itself in mortal danger.

But the changes in foreign policy posed an even more direct threat in the Soviet view, for an independent Czechoslovak foreign policy would eventually have jeopardized the Soviet Union's political, military and ideological hegemony over Eastern Europe. Indeed, in the summer of 1968 there were already signs that Prague, Bucharest, and Belgrade were preparing to pursue a common foreign policy, reminiscent of the Little Entente of the interwar period.[35] Such a new nucleus of power whose driving force would most likely be Titoist Yugoslavia would be a permanent challenge to the Soviet Union's political hegemony in the area. A new Little Entente by its geographic position would have split Eastern Europe into parts, thus isolating politically and diplomatically the Kremlin's most valued fief, East Germany. Finally, there was indeed ample evidence that if developments that began in East Europe in the first half of 1968 had continued the Warsaw Pact would at best have been weakened and at worst it might well have been dissolved entirely within a few years.

Ever since its establishment, the Warsaw Pact has served a twofold purpose. At the time of its conception, it was designed as a defensive military alliance in response to NATO and to West German rearmament. Its second purpose was to serve as a political tool furthering the integration of Eastern Europe. Only in the late 1960's did the Soviet Union transform the Pact into a coercive mechanism which has enabled "the Soviet leadership to keep a restless and explosive conglomeration of states under the influence of Moscow."[36] Indeed the intervention in Czechoslovakia unmistakably demonstrated that the unity and survival of the Pact has become the *conditio sine qua non* of the Soviet East European relations. For this aspect it was not a popular alliance system among those who were members. When Czechoslovakia's General Prchlik called for a thorough revision of the Pact and on the same day Rumania's Ceausescu

35. Most indicative to the possible emergence of an embryonic Little Entente were Tito's press conference, reprinted in *Rude Pravo*, August 10, 1968, and the communiqué issued after his visit to Prague. For the text of the communiqué, see *Rude Pravo*, August 11, 1968. Even more outspoken on the issue of "cooperation on all levels" was the *Communiqué* issued after Ceausescu's visit between August 15 and 17. For the text see *Europa Archiv*, Vol. 23, No. 18 (September, 1968), pp. D424–6.
36. With regard to the changing role of the Warsaw Pact, see especially Roman Kolkowitz, "Spezifischer Funktionswechsel des Warschauer Paktes," *Aussenpolitik*, Vol. 20, No. 1, pp. 5–23.

referred to it as an "instrument of intervention" the Soviet Union could clearly read the handwriting on the wall. A little over a month later combined forces of Poland, East Germany, Hungary, Bulgaria and the Soviet Union invaded Czechoslovakia and put a sudden end to the gallant and unprecedented experimental course upon which the nation's own Communist Party had embarked.

Justification of the Invasion of Czechoslovakia

Viewed within the narrow context of East European politics, the armed intervention and continuous military presence of the Soviet Union in Czechoslovakia proved to be only a temporary and in the long run inadequate stop-gap. At the time of this writing, it is safe to say that in Czechoslovakia and all over Eastern Europe the forces pressing for change are more alive than ever before, and that the orthodox communists are fighting a losing battle. At the same time the invasion did create an entirely new situation in Eastern Europe, the implications of which for the future will be of utmost importance for Europe in general and for West Germany in particular.

There are several aspects of the forceful solution of the East European crisis which deserve close attention. First among them, and for the immediate future of Eastern Europe probably the most important, is the fact that the invasion of Czechoslovakia placed Soviet-East European relations on an entirely new basis. The intervention itself must have brought home to the East European societies, including their reform-minded Communists, that the age-old saying, *extra ecclesiam nulla salus*, is as valid today for Moscow as it was for the Inquisition at the time of Galileo. Even more important is the fact that due to the intervention and to its subsequent justification, the status of the East European countries within the "Socialist Camp" underwent a retrogressive change. In contrast to their complete satellite status under Stalin, and to that of their limited independence under Khrushchev, the post-invasion status of the erstwhile satellites could be best described as that of protectorates in which the characteristics of vassalage are dominant.

Moreover, subsequent to and as justification for the occupation of Czechoslovakia, the Soviet Union developed a new theory of intervention designed to strengthen its hegemonial claims over Eastern Europe. There was never any argument in the Kremlin over the necessity of curbing the process of liberalization in Czechoslovakia, only a dispute about the methods to be employed. However, when the decision in favor of the armed intervention was made, presumably in May at the Moscow meeting of the five prospective invaders, its justification became necessary. Immediately prior to the intervention two statements were issued which unmistakably indicated that henceforth the domestic political development of any one communist regime would be considered as the collective concern of all other communist states.[37] On July 14 and 15 the Party and government heads of East Germany, Poland, and the USSR, Bulgaria and Hungary held a conference in Warsaw where, in the absence of Czechoslovakia, the domestic developments in that country and their implications for the other Socialist states were discussed. In a stinging letter[38] the five participants warned their Czech comrades about the danger of their country being diverted from socialism by domestic reaction nourished by the forces of outside imperialism.

The orthodox communist assertion that any liberalization of a communist party can be attributed only to the successful machinations of imperialism is not a new phenomenon. After all, in their time Tito and Imre Nagy were both branded as lackeys of imperialism. Moreover, the concern of an Ulbricht or that of a Gomulka over the possible emergence of a genuine democracy in a neighboring communist country is quite understandable. However, the five self-appointed judges at Warsaw went much further than mere accusations. The state-

37. For the sake of accuracy it should be noted that the idea of collective concern presaging collective action did develop much earlier than the Czech crisis. For a good short discussion of the issue, see Theodor Schweisfurth, "Moskauer Doktrin und sozialistischer Internationalismus," *Aussenpolitik*, Vol. 19, No. 12 (December, 1968), pp. 710–19, especially pp. 711 ff.
38. See "Gemeinsamer Brief an der kommunistischen Partei der Tschechoslovakei," *Neues Deutschland*, No. 197, July 18, 1968, reprinted in *Europa Archiv*, Vol. 23, No. 16 (August 1968), pp. D388–92. For the answer of the Czechoslovakian Central Committee, see "Czechoslovak Reply" (text rejecting criticism by others in the East European bloc), *The New York Times*, July 19, 1968, pp. C12–13.

ment saying that "There exists a situation which undermines the bases of socialism in Czechoslovakia and threatens the collective vital interests of the other Socialist countries,"[39] clearly indicated that by July, 1968, in the eyes of the five the domestic political developments in Czechoslovakia ceased to be an exclusively internal matter. Moreover, in order to avoid any misunderstanding about the future intentions of the rump communist conclave, the statement contained a serious warning: "These [developments] are not only of your concern. They are the collective concern of all Communist Parties and of all states bound together by alliances of friendship and cooperation."[40] Finally, the letter ended with a reference to those communist forces "which are in the position to defend the socialist order and to defeat the anti-socialist forces,"[41] a clear allusion to the inadequacy of the Czechoslovak leadership.

These statements, as well as the general thrust of the letter which described the Czech developments as counter-revolutionary, clearly indicated a new development in bloc thinking in at least three respects. First, any liberalization of the domestic political and economic structure of a communist country, and any flexibility in its foreign policy is subject to the veto of the bloc. Second, any such action, even if initiated and facilitated by the Party itself, would henceforth be considered as a threat to the security of the whole bloc. Finally, the letter indicated that by July, 1968, if not earlier, the orthodox members of the Warsaw Pact had endorsed the Soviet principle of the primacy of the interests of "proletarian-socialist internationalism." It was then a small matter to turn this unilaterally established right to veto into an obligation to intervene in order to save the vital interests of the Socialist Commonwealth. This occurred about two weeks later in Bratislava at a conference of six Warsaw Pact members, including Czechoslovakia. For the superficial observer the joint Bratislava Declaration[42] issued after the conference would appear as a

39. "Gemeinsamer Brief . . . ," *op. cit.*, p. D391.
40. *Ibid.*, p. 389.
41. *Ibid.*, p. 392.
42. "Gemeinsame Erklärung der kommunistischen und Arbeiterparteien der Sowjetunion, Bulgariens, der DDR, Polens, Ungarns und der Tschecho-

somewhat repetitious expression of communist unity. However, on closer scrutiny it is a declaration of war on the internal and external enemies of the "socialist order." As pointed out earlier, the Bucharest, Karlovy Vary and Budapest conferences were primarily designed by the Soviet Union for the establishment of a common front against imperialism. In this respect the results of the Bratislava conference did not represent a new stage of intra-bloc development. Nor did references to increased vigilance against the imperialistic forces inject any new element into communist thinking. The important and for the immediate future of Eastern Europe decisive stipulations of the Declaration were contained in those passages which dealt with the evolution of the communist system and with the defense of its achievements.

With regard to the problem of the future evolution of the communist system several aspects of the Bratislava Declaration deserve attention. While at Bratislava the inevitability of changes in the system was recognized and accepted, their scope was delimited in advance in at least three important ways. First, in the future any improvement of the communist system "will have to correspond to the principles of democratic centralism,"[43] thus strengthening the power of decision making of the highest Party organs. Second, the communist parties in their efforts for improvements can pay attention to their specific national requirements. However, in order to avoid the repetition of the Czechoslovakian experience, at Bratislava the iron law governing any prospective reform movements was laid down in the following sentence: "Historical experience has convinced the fraternal parties that advancement on the road of Socialism and Communism is possible only in accordance with the general laws of the construction of the socialist society. . . ."[44] The real implications of this stipulation cannot be missed. Its allusion to historical experience clearly established the supremacy of the Soviet way toward socialism as the only example for any prospective reform movement in the "socialist camp,"

slovakei nach ihrer Konferenz in Pressburg am 3. August, 1968," *Europa Archiv*, Vol. 23, No. 16 (August, 1968), pp. D401–4.
43. *Ibid.*, p. D402.
44. *Loc. cit.*

thus relegating the national requirements of the East European societies to the second or third place. Moreover, implicit in the stipulation was the warning that any deviation from the Soviet example would henceforth be considered as a heresy which in turn would constitute a threat to the security of the bloc.

While the stipulations concerning the evolution of communism may have been open to different interpretations, the passage describing the obligations to defend the "socialist achievements" left little doubt about the intentions of the orthodox communists assembled at Bratislava. After a list of the accomplishments achieved since World War II through the relentless common efforts of the "progressive nations," one finds the quintessence of the Bratislava Declaration in the following sentence: "It is the *collective* international obligation of all socialist states to support, strengthen and to *defend* these achievements."[45] [Italics added.] The sentence speaks for itself. If the democratization process in Czechoslovakia with all of its internal and external implications constituted a threat to the collective security of the socialist camp (as it undoubtedly did in the eyes of the Soviet hardliners along with Ulbricht and Gomulka), the only defense against this danger was a collective action, if necessary by the use of force.

The relevant passages of the Bratislava Declaration were actually used as one of the pretexts for the armed intervention of Czechoslovakia.[46] However, although these passages served as the justification of the practice, they were still insufficient to provide a solid basis for a new theory of intervention which the Soviet Union was determined to establish. The hiatus was quickly filled. Subsequent to the occupation a series of articles appeared both in the Soviet Union and, interestingly, in Hungary[47] which advanced the final Soviet version of "prole-

45. *Ibid.*, p. D402.
46. The fact that this part of the Bratislava Declaration was used as a partial justification for the August 21 invasion is clearly seen in the following quotation: "According to the obligations accepted at Bratislava . . . the governments of the USSR and [those of] other allied nations decided to render . . . the necessary help to the fraternal Czechoslovakian nation." Editorial in *Pravda*, August 22, 1968.
47. The most prominent among them was S. Kovalov, "Suverenitat i internationalnye objazannosti socialisticeski stran," *Pravda*, September 26, 1968, p. 4. For the English text see *The Current Digest of the Soviet Press*, Vol.

tarian-socialist internationalism" and a concomitant reinterpretation of the concepts of sovereignty and self-determination. The principle underlying this new doctrine[48] is that the international relations of the communist countries, while secondarily subject to the general norms of international law, are to be primarily governed by the specific laws of "socialist internationalism" which rests on a twofold consideration. On the one hand it is anchored in the brotherly friendship, close cooperation and mutual assistance of all communist parties. On the other hand, it obliges the members of the socialist community to focus their attention primarily on the requirements of "the world-wide system of socialism" along with the specific demands and characteristics of their national environments.[49] It logically follows from this order of priority that no indigenous Party is permitted to make any decision contradictory to the interests of either the other socialist states, or to those of the allegedly "world-wide system of socialism." The direct consequence of this communist logic is the fact that every Communist Party, especially if it is a governing one, is responsible to all other communist parties as well as to the world movement of which the Soviet Union is the self-proclaimed leader. Thus, the ex post facto theoretical justification of the Warsaw Pact invasion of Czechoslovakia seems to have established at least three new norms. First, by making "socialist internationalism" the governing principle of inter-communist state relations it superseded the norms of general international law. Second, by subordinating the national interests of the

20, No. 39 (October 16, 1968), pp. 10–12. See also Nikola Shawi, "Internationalism and the Cause of Peace," *Pravda*, October 23, 1968, p. 4; for the English text see *The Current Digest of the Soviet Press*, Vol. 20, No. 43 (November, 1968), pp. 16–17. In the Hungarian press see especially Kádár's speech on October 24, 1968, full text given in *Népszabadság*, October 24, 1968, pp. 2–3, Cf. "Reális lehetöségek" (editorial), *Magyar Nemzet*, August 29, 1968, p. 1, and István Szirmai's speech immediately following the intervention in *Magyar Nemzet*, August 28, 1968, p. 3.

48. The topic has already produced a considerable amount of literature. See especially Theodor Schweisfurth, "Moskauer Doktrin und sozialisticher Internationalismus," *Aussenpolitik*, Vol. 19, No. 12 (December, 1968), pp. 710–19; see also Harald Lauen, "Osteuropa unter dem Zugriff der Hegemonialmacht," *Europa Archiv*, Vol. 23, No. 20 (October, 1968), pp. 735–43. Cf. R. Kolkowitz, *op. cit.*, especially pp. 16 ff.

49. Th. Schweisfurth, *op. cit.*, pp. 712 ff.

indigeneous communist parties to the overall interests of the community, and by establishing the former's responsibility to the latter, it created a new Soviet version of interdependence and limited sovereignty. Finally, by making "mutual assistance" obligatory (even if the assistance is not solicited) the principle of "socialist internationalism" eliminated the concepts of "intervention" and "aggression" from the communist vocabulary with respect to another communist state.

In addition to these three considerations there are two other aspects of the new theory which deserve some attention. In an article entitled "The Sovereignty and International Obligations of Socialist Countries," Soviet writer S. Kovalov took great pains to advance the thesis that the independence and international standing of the individual socialist state is derived from and preserved by the strength of the entire socialist community and even more so by the formidable power of its main pillar, the Soviet Union.[50] The final arbiter of what does and does not conform to the tenets of "proletarian-socialist internationalism" was, obviously, to be the USSR. The second aspect is only indirectly connected with the new theory, and concerns the changed nature of the Warsaw Pact, although the two are inextricably connected. The fact that the Pact was used as a collective vehicle against another communist state not only changed its basic functions, but also fundamentally altered the relationship among its members. By limiting the sovereignty of its vassals and by arrogating the right to be the exclusive interpreter of ideological purity or heresy, Moscow destroyed that little equality which might have existed among the members of the Pact. At the time of this writing, it is probably not premature to advance the tentative conclusion that the Warsaw Pact in its previous form, i.e., an alliance in which the USSR occupied the place of a *primus inter pares* while other members enjoyed a certain degree of independence, has ceased to exist.

Bonn and Moscow

Soviet post-intervention propaganda has attempted to make

50. S. Kovalov, *op. cit.*, p. 11.

the occupation of Czechoslovakia appear as a solely internal affair of the socialist camp. However, this Soviet assertion is untenable. This proposition was refuted prior to the invasion by the Kremlin's increasingly hardening foreign policy posture toward Bonn. Subsequent to the events, it has been refuted by the new doctrine of "socialist internationalism." On July 11, 1968, the Soviet government published a series of *aide mémoires* and notes covering the exploratory diplomatic conversations between Moscow and Bonn on the issue of the renunciation of the use of force.[51] The mere fact that the Soviet government made public the contents of confidential diplomatic talks in itself suggested Soviet disinterest in any agreement with West Germany. Furthermore, the language of some of the Soviet notes, and especially the texts of the draft-declarations unmistakably revealed the unbridgeable gap beween Moscow's and Bonn's interpretation of the issue. For Bonn an eventual exchange of declarations barring force from the East European political scene could have made the task of West Germany's diplomacy in that area less tortuous. By contrast it was apparently Moscow's intention to use any agreement on the issue with Bonn as an instrument through which the latter would irrevocably accept the East European status quo.

It also appears from the *aide mémoires* that as early as 1967 a mere acceptance of the status quo would not have satisfied the Soviet Union. The references to Article 107, and especially to Article 53, of the UN Charter[52] left little doubt about the real thrust of Soviet intentions. On the one hand, they made it unmistakably clear that any agreement between West Germany and the Soviet Union concerning the renunciation of the use of force would have been one among absolutely unequal partners. On the other hand, Moscow's insistence on the applicability of the measures contained in both Articles "against the renewal of aggressive policies on the part of a former enemy state"[53]

---

51. For the texts of the most important Soviet and West German notes, see "Der deutsch-sowjetischer Meinungsaustausch zur Frage des Gewaltverzichts," *Europa Archiv*, Vol. 23, No. 16 (August 25, 1968), pp. D361–86.
52. See especially the paragraphs discussing the rights and obligations of the former Occupying Powers, *ibid.*, pp. D366 ff.
53. *Ibid.*, p. D367.

clearly expressed the Soviet determination to retain its questionable prerogative of intervention in West German domestic affairs.

The question whether or not the stipulations of Articles 107 and 53 are still applicable to West Germany is beside the point. One could even argue whether or not the Soviet insistence on the theory of "two German states" has made the same Articles obsolete. However, if one considers the fact that in Moscow's interpretation the emergence of the new Right in West Germany is a prelude to a new German aggression, or that Bonn's continuous membership in NATO actually pre-empts the meaning of aggressive policy, one can only conclude that an agreement between Bonn and Moscow on the issue of the renunciation of the use of force would have produced only one result. While Bonn's acceptance of the status quo, including the special status of West Berlin, would have been unconditional, the Soviet Union would have succeeded in institutionalizing a nonexistent or at least highly dubious right of unilateral use of force against the Federal Republic. That this interpretation of Soviet intentions is more than a conjecture has been demonstrated after the occupation of Czechoslovakia by extensive comments on the issue by the Soviet press.[54]

Moreover, the last Soviet note,[55] issued only a few weeks before the occupation of Czechoslovakia, must be regarded not only as unequivocal testimony of Soviet intransigence in the German question but also as a document clearly revealing the Kremlin's position on the unchangeability of the East European political and ideological status quo. Sentences such as "there will never be a return to the Reich," or "there are neither direct or indirect avenues toward a revision of the European boundaries"[56] left little doubt about Soviet determination to

54. See especially Vladle Kuznetsov, "With a Long-Range Aim," *Pravda*, September 18, 1968, p. 5. Most informative on the Soviet view concerning the applicability of Articles 107 and 53 is L. Volodin, "At the Beck of the Revanchists," *Isvestia*, September 20, 1968, p. 1. For the English texts of both articles see *The Current Digest of the Soviet Press*, Vol. 20, No. 38, pp. 15–16.
55. "Der deutsch-sowjetischer Meinungsaustausch . . . ," *op. cit.* pp. D378–86.
56. *Ibid.*, pp. D380 ff.

maintain the political structure of Central and Eastern Europe. The repetitious references to the "unity of the Socialist states" and to their existence as a "guarantee of European security" indicated the degree of importance attached by the Soviet Union to the permanency of the ideological status quo in Eastern Europe.

Finally, it would be a gross error to assume that the new Soviet doctrine of "limited sovereignty" with all its implications was designed exclusively to place inter-communist relations on a new basis. It is true that its primary function was to re-establish and to maintain Soviet hegemony over Eastern Europe. It is also true that the increased emphasis on "socialist internationalism" intended to provide the socialist camp with the much needed inner cohesion. However, it is also evident that since late 1968 the incorporation of the class struggle in the ideological context of Soviet-style international law represents a threat of anticipatory justification of interventions in the affairs of non-communist states. If, as Kovalov maintains, the rules and norms of international law "are subject to the laws of class-struggle and to those of social development,"[57] the applicability of the right of intervention cannot remain restricted to the socialist nations because the assertion of a general "Socialist international law of nations" in terms of class distinction offers an ideological or theoretical basis for uninhibited interventions throughout the world. Consequently, if the Soviet Union's right of intervention exists at all times and is applicable to all places, the doctrine represents a specific threat to the Federal Republic (or at least blocks closer relations).

To be sure, the threat is more psychological than physical in spite of the by now permanent military presence of the Soviet Union along most of the Eastern borders of the Federal Republic. Yet one cannot escape the feeling that the forceful solution of the Czechoslovakian crisis and its posthumous justification were directed not only against the truly progressive forces in Eastern Europe but also against West Germany's *Deutschland* and *Ostpolitik*, which in August, 1968, was brought to a temporary standstill.

57. Kovalov, *op. cit.*, pp. 11 ff.

8

a new "ostpolitik"— the limitations of a foreign policy

The brutal 1968 Warsaw Pact intervention and the new doctrine it produced seem to have had an unexpected stabilizing effect on European politics. As one American commentator pointed out, the Europeans have come to regard the post-Czechoslovakian era as conducive to "flexible diplomacy" and as an "opportunity to change the political face of Europe."[1] Soviet behavior during and after the invasion encouraged individual Western European states to approach the Kremlin on a bilateral basis, in the style made familiar by de Gaulle.

In France and elsewhere, the determination to continue from *détente* through *entente* to *cooperation* was not shaken by the invasion of Czechoslovakia. For de Gaulle and likeminded statesmen, these events were a "traffic accident" which should not stand in the way of a European settlement.

1. Laszlo Hadik, "The Process of Detente in Europe," *Orbis*, Vol. XIII, No. 4 (Winter, 1970), pp. 1008–28.

German politicians concurred, for neither France nor Germany regarded the invasion and the Brezhnev Doctrine as a display of Russian hostility or a threat to themselves, but rather as an internal imperial gambit for the maintenance of Soviet-style stability within the Socialist Commonwealth. Consequently, both France and Germany took advantage of the post-1968 stability to greatly expand their relations with the Soviet Union. American silence and inaction indicated that the United States also tacitly accepted the Soviet contention that preservation of the status quo and continuation of *détente* were inseparable.

The 1969 elections to the West German parliament and the emergence of a new ruling coalition of the Social Democrats and Free Democrats allowed the formulation of a more vigorous Eastern policy which made limited rapprochement with the Soviet Union possible.

The CDU/CSU registered minimal losses with 46.1 percent of the vote, down from 47.1 percent in 1966. The Social Democrats registered more than a 3 percent gain over 1966 by polling most of the votes cast. The Free Democratic Party (FDP) lost, barely escaping the 5 percent cut-off for representation in the Federal Assembly, with only 5.8 percent.[2] The CDU/CSU was thus still the strongest single Party in West Germany, followed closely by the SPD, with the Free Democrats trailing far behind both. An SPD-FDP coalition was virtually the only one possible in 1969. Prior to the election both the CDU/CSU and the SPD had declared that they favored dissolving the Great Coalition. Moreover, from the summer of 1969 on through the campaign, the FDP made its preference for coalition with the SPD clear — a preference which probably cost them over one-third of their middle-class votes.

This opportunity to be the senior partner in a new coalition was willingly accepted by Willy Brandt and Herbert Wehner, and the Coalition was established with remarkable speed.

---

2. One may also mention the NDP which with 4.3 percent of the votes remained outside of the confines of the *Bundestag*. As a result of this election, followed by an inner-party struggle which lessened the appeal of the NPD, the Party since 1969 has ceased to be a serious political factor on the Federal as well as on the *Länder* level.

Thirty-one years had elapsed since a Social Democrat had held the post of Chancellor under the Weimar Republic. The party had spent seventeen years in opposition followed by three years as the junior member in the Great Coalition. At last it occupied the seat of power, but its majority was slim; its partner weak and notoriously poorly disciplined and its opposition — at least in the beginning — strongly united. Extra-parliamentary opposition on the extreme left continued its demagogic tactics uninterrupted against the new "establishment" and, last but not least, expectations for what the new government could accomplish were dangerously high. The new government felt obliged to win some important success rather early on, lest its position deteriorate. Because the new partners' positions were rather far apart with regard to domestic preferences, the Brandt-Scheel government turned its attention to foreign policy in general and to new overtures to Eastern Europe in particular.[3]

While the Coalition's Western policy did not contain any new elements, its declaration of intent toward the East was a curious mixture of continuity and change. The expressed need for "... an understanding with the East" and the drive "toward a peace in the fullest sense of the word with the peoples of the Soviet Union and Eastern Europe" and the willingness to offer "a mutual renunciation of the use of force ..." including the GDR[4] pointed toward a continuation of the Kiesinger-Brandt policies. The intent to pursue a policy of intensified trade, technological cooperation and cultural exchange, and to reach an understanding with Czechoslovakia did not represent a change from former policy platforms either. What was strikingly new in the government's Eastern policy was its determination to transform previous two-sided monologues into real dialogues and to initiate new talks wherever possible. To this end, near the end of his exposé, Willy Brandt came forward with a set of concrete proposals. Of utmost importance among them was the determination to answer the USSR's *aide mémoire* on the issue of the renunciation of the use of

3. "Regierungserklärung von Bundeskanzler Willy Brandt vor dem Deutschen Bundestag am 28. Oktober, 1969," *Bulletin*, No. 132, October 29, 1969, pp. 1121–8.
4. *Ibid.*, p. 1126.

force, and to propose a fixed date for the reopening of diplomatic conversations on this topic. Equally important was the declaration to initiate preliminary conversations with Poland along the lines of the Gomulka speech in May, 1969. In addition to the above issues, and probably to demonstrate his sincerity, the Chancellor announced the government's willingness to sign the Treaty of Nuclear Non-proliferation, which had long been a thorn in the flesh of the East European communist states.[5] With these proposals the course of Brandt's Eastern policy was set in a manner which seemed to ensure maximum flexibility for its execution.

Revitalizing its Eastern policy automatically required a re-examination of the government's German policy. Here the Coalition was rather limited. Faced with Ulbricht's "all or nothing" approach toward an intra-German normalization, and the certainty that any far-reaching concessions would be met with a fierce domestic opposition (even within the FDP), the Coalition was confronted with a formidable problem in attempting to bring the East German regime to the conference table. Brandt reiterated all the offers of former West German governments, including negotiations on the governmental level leading to contractual agreements, intensified intra-German trade, agreement on the mutual renunciation of the use of force, etc.[6] Moreover, as if to demonstrate the prospective advantages of Pankow's eventual conciliatory attitudes toward Bonn, Brandt added that "with regard to the international position of the GDR our attitude and that of our friends ultimately depends on the [future] behavior of East Berlin."[7] This statement unmistakably implied that Pankow's consent to a contractual normalization of intra-German relations could eventually end the isolation of the GDR *vis-à-vis* the West and result in Pankow's acceptance in international organizations on an equal basis. This much Brandt could do, thus promising much more to the Ulbricht regime than had anyone of his predecessors. However, what the new Chancellor could not promise to Pankow was the long desired de jure recognition. It is true that

5. *Ibid.*, p. 1128.
6. *Loc. cit.*
7. *Ibid.*, p. 1129.

in saying that "in Germany there exist two states" Brandt officially acknowledged a political reality which has existed ever since 1949. But he immediately stated the new government's determination not to recognize the other part of Germany "under international law, for [the two states] are not foreign countries to one another" and as such their relations could be regulated only "through special arrangements."[8] At least on the surface, then, the changes in the Coalition's foreign policy program seemed to be minimal.

The first breakthrough in Brandt's *Ostpolitik* came, however, shortly after the announcement of the Coalition's governmental program. On December 8, 11, and 23, 1969, the West German ambassador was permitted to engage in preliminary conversations with Moscow, with a view toward "normalizing" Russo-German relations including the most important issue, a prospective agreement on the mutual renunciation of the use of force. Little more than a year after Czechoslovakia, the Soviet Union, which had brought the Great Coalition's Eastern policy to a standstill, was willing to reconsider its former intransigence.

The first initiative to exchange declarations renouncing the use of force with regard to Eastern Europe came from Bonn in 1966 in the so-called *Friedensnote* (Peace note) of the Erhard government, saying that the Federal Republic is ready "to exchange formal declarations with the Soviet Union and ... with any other East European states, if it desires [to do so], in which [declaration] each state renounces the use of force" as an instrument of settling international disputes.[9] A few months later the new Chancellor, Kurt Kiesinger, not only repeated the same offer but also extended it to East Germany, saying that Bonn "is ready to include in this offer the unsolved problem of Germany's division."[10] Diplomatic conversations on the topic started early in 1967 and continued until July, 1968, when Moscow, committing a gross indiscretion in diplomatic

---

8. *Loc. cit.*
9. "Zirkularnote der deutschen Bundesregierung zur deutschen Friedens-politik," *Bulletin*, No. 42, March 26, 1966, pp. 329–31.
10. To this see Kiesinger's "Regierungserklärung . . . ," *op. cit.*, pp. D15 ff.

intercourse, published their contents.[11] It is not necessary to discuss all details of the conversations which have been amply documented by Bonn.[12] Suffice it to say that between 1967 and 1968 Moscow maintained the most intransigent attitude toward Bonn with regard to this particular topic. The Kremlin not only insisted on its alleged right to intervene in the affairs of West Germany under the so-called "enemy states" articles of the UN Charter (Art. 53 and 107), but it also implicitly maintained that such an intervention would be justified by the re-emergence of fascism, militarism and imperialism in West Germany. Thus by July, 1967, when *Izvestia* published the exchange of notes (to be sure, only five weeks prior to the Czechoslovakian invasion) the positions of Moscow and Bonn seemed to be as irreconcilable as ever.

From early spring, 1969, there had been signs that Moscow wished to escape from its self-created political impasse. The first visible indication of change came in March at the Warsaw Pact Conference in Budapest. In contrast to former conferences the communiqué issued at Budapest differed in two important points with regard to the Federal Republic. First, what had formerly been fixed pre-conditions for normalization, such as the recognition of the GDR and the a priori acceptance of the status quo, were now labeled as only "advisable." Second, the Warsaw Pact members demonstrated a more conciliatory attitude toward Bonn by omitting any references to its alleged fascism, imperialism and aggressive intentions toward Eastern Europe.[13] Even more encouraging to Bonn were certain passages in a speech of Polish Party chief Gomulka, delivered in May, in which the Polish leader definitely indicated his country's

11. For a brief but excellent account of the background to Moscow's changed attitude see: Klaus Mehnert, "Der Moskauer Vertrag," *Osteuropa*, Vol. 20, No. 12 (December 12, 1970), p. 810. See also: Wolfgang Wagner, "Voraussetzungen und Folgen der deutschen Ostpolitik," *Europa Archiv*, Vol. 25, No. 17 (September 10, 1970), pp. 627–36, *passim*.
12. *Die Politik des Gewaltverzichts. Eine Dokumentation der deutschen und sowjetischen Erklärungen zum Gewaltverzicht, 1949 bis Juli 1968* (Presse und Informationsamt der Bundesregierung, Bonn, 1968).
13. For the text of the Budapest Appeal see *Neues Deutschland*, March 18, 1969; also reprinted in *Osteuropa*, Vol. 20, No. 10 (October, 1969,) pp. A690–3.

desire for more normal relations.[14] These encouraging signs were not lost on Bonn. On July 4, the Great Coalition presented an *aide mémoire* to the Soviet Union indicating its willingness to reopen conversations on the renunciation of the use of force. As early as July 10 this offer drew a positive answer from Soviet Foreign Minister Gromyko in a speech before the Supreme Soviet and was followed up by an equally positive response on September 13.[15]

All these conciliatory gestures of course were addressed to the Great Coalition, but that summer the Soviet Union made it clear that it would be gratified if the upcoming elections led to a change in Bonn. In July SPD and FDP delegations, including Walter Scheel, traveled to Moscow and were given ostentatiously preferential treatment.[16] These Soviet overtures to the leftist-liberals from Bonn were tantamount to intervention in the West Germany election campaign. Soviet intentions behind this friendly facade were far from clear, however.

The bloody conflict with China at the Ussuri River may have prompted Moscow to improve its position in the West between the two communist giants. The possibility that a protracted armed conflict on its Eastern borders might combine with insecurity of the Western perimeters of its European empire must have been sobering. Immediately after the skirmishes at the Sino-Soviet border the propaganda campaign against the election of the President of the Federal Republic of Germany

14. "Rede des Ersten Sekretars der Polnischen Arbeiterpartei, Wladyslaw Gomulka in Warschau am 17. Mai," *Europa Archiv*, Vol. 24, No. 13, pp. 313–20. That Warsaw, and therefore Moscow, along with the other East European capitals would welcome an SPD-dominated government in Bonn was first implied when Gomulka referred to the SPD as a potentially more realistic partner in the eventually forthcoming East-West conversations; see *ibid.*, pp. 317 ff. Even more indicative of a benevolent anticipation of an SPD government was the fact that in March the chief ideologue of the Kremlin, Suslov, actually exonerated the SPD's behavior during the 1930's thus changing long-standing ideological concepts of Moscow and virtually directing the other East European states to follow suit. In this regard see Mehnert, "Der Moskauer Vertrag," *op. cit.*, pp. 812 ff.

15. "Dokumente zur Ostpolitik der Bundesregierung Deutschland," *Europa Archiv*, Vol. 25, No. 8 (April 25, 1970), pp. D175–202.

16. In this regard see the not entirely sympathetic articles, "Liebesgrüsse aus Moskau," *Der Spiegel*, Vol. 23, No. 31 (July 28, 1968), pp. 23–24, and "FDP auf Stellensuche," *ibid.*, p. 24. Cf. "Mit einer Stimme Mehrheit in die Regierung," *ibid.*, Vol. 23, No. 32, pp. 26–31.

in West Berlin was abruptly canceled. Obtaining Bonn's eventual agreement to the renunciation of the use of force would by definition involve accepting the European status quo and this would have provided the USSR with a breathing period in which to consolidate its position within Eastern Europe. The Soviet Union's need for a massive Western and especially West German economic engagement in Soviet economic development undoubtedly played its part. Nor should one dismiss the possibility that Soviet policy makers felt an eventual Russo-German rapprochement would weaken Bonn's ties to the West and could, perhaps, retard the process of West European integration.

Bonn's overtures to Pankow were initially less promising and in their results much less productive. They were even counterproductive. If the Brandt-Scheel coalition hoped for even a minimum of reciprocity from the GDR in turn for accepting the "two states theory" or for the far-reaching concessions which Bonn was obviously prepared to grant, they were disappointed. And if the Russians had hoped that an eventual intra-German normalization could serve as an example for a workable peaceful coexistence between the communist and democratic systems in Europe, they remained equally disillusioned.

Shortly after the establishment of the Brandt-Scheel coalition, Herbert Wehner said with regard to the intra-German relations that "if necessary, we will have to scratch for the smallest success with our fingernails."[17] As if to frame the truth of these words, the Ulbricht regime's response to Bonn was slow, uncompromising and more hostile than ever. Pankow recognized the change in Bonn's political leadership but did not take cognizance of the change in the policy itself. The old demands were repeated almost in the same terms as before. Instead of acknowledging Brandt's acceptance of the two German states as tangible evidence of Bonn's good intentions, it was interpreted as another form of discrimination especially since it was coupled with the promise of "contractual agreements of special character." In December Ulbricht himself made a speech be-

17. Theo Sommer, "Rückblick auf ein 'deutsches Jahr'," *Die Zeit*, February 2, 1971, p. 5.

fore the Central Committee of the SED, and there was no trace of any desire to compromise with Bonn. On the contrary, according to Ulbricht the process of "normalization" depended on recognition under international law, on treaties to be concluded between two sovereign independent states, on the abolition on Bonn's part of any legislation discriminatory toward the GDR and on contractually agreed non-interference in one another's domestic affairs.[18] Furthermore, as if to demonstrate that Bonn could hope for no concessions whatever from the GDR, Ulbricht denied even the existence of the German nation, differentiating between an imperialist, anti-socialist and militarist Federal Republic and a peace-loving Socialist GDR. The attempt to construct a "common national roof" over the two German states was an illusion.[19] Yet, while positing these demands — which to be sure were minimum — Ulbricht was careful to seem to leave the door open for prospective negotiations, stating that "we also desire a peaceful coexistence and a *step by step* construction of good neighborliness, arrived at through mutually binding international treaties."[20] However, in the same breath Ulbricht made establishment of the "good neighborhood" dependent on the growth of "peace-loving forces" (i.e. anti-democratic forces) in West Germany which were to be furthered by the new Social Democratic government itself. Thus Ulbricht arrogated to himself the right of domestic interference which he so categorically denied to Bonn.

In Ulbricht's interpretation the term "negotiation" was still equivalent with a demand for unconditional capitulation by Bonn, however. Ulbricht's intention to demand nothing less than a total surrender became apparent when he presented the West German president with a draft treaty[21] and proposed to begin negotiations leading to its acceptance in January, 1970.

18. "Rede des Staatsvorsitzenden der DDR und Ersten Sekretärs des ZK der SED, Walter Ulbricht vor dem Zentralkomitee der Partei am 13. December, 1969," *Neues Deutschland*, No. 345, December 14, 1969; reprinted in *Europa Archiv*, Vol. 25, No. 8, pp. D187–90.
19. *Ibid.*, p. D189.   20. *Ibid.*, p. D190; italics added.
21. For the official text of Ulbricht's proposal see "Draft of a 'Treaty on the Establishment of Relations between the German Democratic Republic and the Federal Republic of Germany on a Basis of Equality'," in *Kassel, May 21,*

On reading the articles of the draft one wonders whether or not Pankow actually expected an immediate rejection from Bonn hoping that it could then place the onus on the Coalition for having deliberately sabotaged the issue of normalization between the two German states. The terms of the draft were painstakingly precise in calling for the establishment of normal relations "on the basis of universally recognized principles and norms of international law" (Article 1); for the recognition and inviolability of the frontiers between the two German states along with the other East European boundaries (Article 2); for the exchange of ambassadors (Article 5); and for the acceptance of West Berlin as an independent political entity (Article 7). Nor did Ulbricht's draft leave any doubt as to how the GDR envisaged the proposed "normal" relations. Article 3 called upon Bonn to "rescind laws and other normative acts" which may be discriminating against East Germany "without delay." And to ensure the right of domestic interference of the GDR the same Article enjoined Bonn "to refrain from any discrimination of the other party" in the future. Finally the most important message of the draft treaty was conveyed to Bonn by an omission, for there was no reference whatsoever to the German nation, indicating that once the treaty was accepted even this last — and in 1969 already questionable — common denominator would be eliminated.

At the end of 1969, at least from his own point of view, Ulbricht had every reason to be satisfied. As one West German commentator put it, with his speech, with his letter to President Heinemann and with the draft treaty the old "apparatchik" had successfully, though temporarily, stopped Bonn's attempts at an intra-German compromise.[22] For even if the Coalition had inched toward an eventual recognition of the GDR, this was not done to perpetuate the division of the nation. On the contrary, even the official acknowledgment of the GDR as a separate political entity — which roughly amounted to a de facto recognition — served only one purpose: namely, to bring

---

A Documentation (Press and Information Office of the Federal Republic of Germany), pp. 81–83.
22. Bernt Conrad, "Ulbricht nutzt seinen Spielraum," *Die Welt*, December 30, 1969.

Pankow to the negotiating table with the purpose of easing the division of Germany.

In December, 1969, Ulbricht successfully destroyed the very cornerstone of this policy. His answer to Bonn's offer of a "qualified recognition" was to demand a final, formal and internationally binding recognition. Ulbricht also made it unmistakably clear that such a recognition would not usher in a period of cooperation between the two German states, but rather that it would serve as the seal of their irrevocable separation. Moreover, as the price for cooperation Ulbricht set other pre-conditions and requirements the fulfillment of which would have made the Federal Republic the vassal of communist Eastern Europe. To mention only a few: Bonn's withdrawal from the Western alliance, a break with the United States, the "demilitarization of West Germany," and a revolutionary change in its socio-economic structure, presumably furthered by the government itself.

It was obvious that these conditions amounted to the total rejection of the "policy of reconciliation" of the Brandt-Scheel government. Less obvious was whether or not Ulbricht acted single-handedly and in contradiction to the general political trends in communist Eastern Europe. Was it possible to believe in 1969 that Ulbricht deliberately misinterpreted the *Westpolitik* of Moscow? Every indication points to the opposite. It should be remembered that Ulbricht has always been the most faithful interpreter of Moscow's policies, because in the ultimate analysis his interests have always been identical with those of Moscow. Furthermore, at the ad hoc Moscow conference in early December, the tactical considerations for the Bloc's Western strategy were ironed out. It is hard to believe that shortly thereafter Ulbricht would deviate from these rules. In and after 1969 Ulbricht has remained the faithful executor of Moscow's *Deutschlandpolitik* which, by putting up a facade of reconciliation, aims not at a genuine "change through rapprochement" but at a "change through unilateral fulfillments" at the end of which the hegemonial position of the Soviet Union in Eastern Europe and its position as *arbiter Germaniae* would be secured.

It was probably this last aspect of Ulbricht's maneuvers

which should have served as a warning to the Brandt-Scheel coalition. That in spite of so much intransigence the government went ahead with its rapprochement policy must be attributed to a variety of factors. First, even as early as the beginning of the new year the government's Eastern policy seems to have reached the point of no return.[23] Second, the Brandt government obviously hoped that an eventual agreement with Moscow would induce the latter to make concessions on the German question. Third, it is probably safe to say that the political survival of the Coalition depended on some success (one is tempted to say on *any* success) in its foreign policy toward the East. Finally, and in this case the Coalition hardly had any alternatives, in 1970 an intra-German dialogue, unpromising as it may have been, had become unavoidable.

Be that as it may, by mid-January the former euphoria of the leftist-liberal coalition was replaced by a great amount of sobriety. Expressions such as "we will have to test the deepest depths of the other side," and "negotiate, if necessary, into the next generation"[24] had now become the *Leitmotiv* of the government. The newly found sobriety was best expressed by the Chancellor himself in his report to the West German Parliament on the "State of the Nation."[25] The report was also characterized by a much harsher tone toward the GDR. While the Chancellor expressed his government's determination to negotiate with Pankow, he also declared what was nonnegotiable for West Germany: the self-determination of the Germans, the de jure recognition of the GDR, the status of Berlin and the rights of the Allies in that city, and the continuous efforts of the Germans to seek their national unity under a European security arrangement.[26] What was further held to be

23. "Bonn-Gefangener der Ostpolitik?" *Neue Zürcher Zeitung*, February 15; see also "Schmale Marge für Brandt," *ibid.*, January 18, 1970.
24. These remarks were made by the leader of the SPD's parliamentary faction, Herbert Wehner, during the first foreign policy debate in the Bundestag. See: *Deutscher Bundestag*, 6. Wahlperiode, Stenographische Berichte, *passim*.
25. "Verpflichtung zur Wahrung der Einheit der deutschen Nation," *Bulletin*, No. 6, January 15, 1970, pp. 49–56. For additional information with respect to the "State of the Nation" message, see "Materialen der Bundesregierung zum Bericht zur Lage der Nation," *Bulletin*, No. 5, Jan. 14, 1970, pp. 33–48.   26. "Verpflichtung . . . ," *op cit.*, p. 52.

non-negotiable was the unity of the German nation. Yet it was exactly this passage in the Chancellor's report which was the most ambiguous. What was missing was a clear-cut differentiation between "state" and "nation" and a clarification of the problem created by the *alleged* unity of the nation and the de facto existence of two states on its territory. It is true that in his speech Brandt carefully avoided the word "reunification." But at the same time he replaced it with "preservation of the unity of the nation" which, according to Brandt, should be the duty of both states on German soil.[27] If one is inclined to think in terms of historical analogies, Brandt's efforts could, perhaps, be compared to past attempts at finding a common, national denominator between Austria and Germany after the former's exclusion from the German Federation in 1866. However, in the Germany of the 1970's not even the notion of "national unity" could have served as a common basis for any kind of unity, cooperation or regulated coexistence between the two exclusive socio-political systems.

The rest, the concrete offers contained in the Chancellor's report, were: willingness to negotiate and to conclude agreements on the governmental level, a promise to respect the domestic political system of the other side, the application of the GDR of all the principles which regulate the relations between states including non-discrimination, and the acceptance of territorial integrity. All these were more or less repetitions of the governmental program. However, as if to remind the other side that the heart of politics is compromise, the Chancellor warned that "a treaty between the GDR and ourselves cannot become a wall of fog"[28] behind which everything remains unchanged. This was a clear-cut reference to one of the main objectives of Brandt's policy: to bring about a more bearable life behind the "bleeding frontier." To be sure, the Chancellor did not spell out what further concessions his government would be willing to make to achieve this objective. But the sentence "the Federal Republic will be willing to consider many other things if such an act will result in a relief in the lives of the people in divided Germany"[29] spoke for itself.

---

27. *Ibid.*, p. 56.   28. *Ibid.*, p. 51.   29. *Ibid.*, p. 55.

Thus Brandt set the course of his "dynamic" German policy. However, the other side had also set its course. Was there, in January, 1970, any hope that Brandt's and Ulbricht's Germany would ever meet at the point of intra-German reconciliation? The sober answer to this question was given by Walter Scheel himself one year later when he said: "We regret that the consequences of our policy are the least felt in the GDR."[30] And in a few days later, in his second message on the state of the German nation, Brandt said: "One is enough to trigger off a crisis, but to maintain the peace the efforts of all are required."[31] These were sober remarks with respect to a year which was supposed to become "the German year." Were the two Germanies able to find some semblance of a common denominator in the interim? Was Willy Brandt able to convince his East German counterpart that since politics is the art of the possible it must be based on mutual compromise?

The answers to these questions are unfortunately negative. The fact that the gap between the two German states remained as wide as before was apparent at the two historic meetings between Willy Brandt and Willi Stoph at Erfurt and Kassel.[32] These meetings were neither negotiations nor were they conversations at the end of which some positive achievements could be registered. They were brutal, direct confrontations between two systems, one of which steadily insisted on the unconditional fulfillment of its total demands while the other side was pressed to retreat from most of its earlier positions step by step. Nothing was solved either in Erfurt or Kassel, nor did these meetings bring eventual solutions any nearer. Nor was there any "break-through" into the promising domain of concession to which the new *Ostpolitik* had looked forward so impatiently. One must agree with Chancellor Brandt that "the

30. "Grundlagen der Aussenpolitik der Bundesregierung; Antwort der Bundesregierung auf eine grosse Anfrage der Fraktionen der SPD und FDP," *Bulletin*, No. 9, January 26, 1971, p. 79.
31. "Bericht der Bundesregierung zur Lage der Nation," *Bulletin*, No. 12, January 26, 1971, p. 106.
32. For a full English documentation of these two meetings see *Erfurt, March 19, 1970, A Documentation*, and *Kassel, May 21, 1970, A Documentation*, both published by the Press and Information Office of the Federal Government, Bonn, 1970.

journey to Erfurt was right, necessary, and useful."[33] But on balance, the negative aspects of these meetings far outweigh the positive achievements.

Willy Brandt went to Erfurt with few illusions[34] and to Kassel with even fewer. Yet even the most pessimistic commentators in the Federal Republic did not expect that he would return from both cities almost empty-handed. The only positive result of the Erfurt meeting was that the parties agreed to meet again in May. At Kassel not even an "agreement to disagree" was reached. Instead, the meetings were postponed indefinitely, calling for a "thinking period" for both sides. The negative results were both implicit and explicit. The fact that a meeting between the heads of the two German governments took place at all implied that the GDR had been recognized at least de facto by Bonn. An official conversation between the West German Chancellor and the East German Prime Minister implied that both actually recognized the other's government and accepted it as an equal partner. Therefore, after Erfurt there was no return for Bonn to its former position of sole spokesman for all Germany. Henceforth, Bonn could not claim to represent the sole model of a free Germany. For all practical purposes at these two meetings East Germany, along with its totalitarian system, was accepted as an equal part and partner.

These confrontations demonstrated that the two systems are irreconcilable and that the obstacles toward a minimum intra-German understanding remain insurmountable. If prior to the first meeting there had existed any hope for at least the semblance of a common language between the negotiating partners, Erfurt and Kassel shattered such expectations. Stoph's hour-long speech was a veritable compendium of clichés.[35] Finally, there was no indication at all either at Erfurt or Kassel that the intra-German confrontations could eventually be turned into real negotiations.

33. See Willy Brandt's report to the Bundestag on March 20, 1970, reprinted in *Erfurt . . .* , *op cit.*, pp. 57 ff.
34. To this see Brandt's opening speech at the Erfurt negotiations in *ibid.*, p. 37.
35. In this regard see "Statement by Willi Stoph, Chairman of the German Democratic Republic's Ministerial Council at the Meeting with Willy

Even the seemingly positive result of Erfurt, the agreement to continue the talks,[36] had its drawbacks. Brandt interpreted Stoph's accepting his invitation to the Federal Republic as a clear indication of the GDR's interest in the continuation of the talks. Brandt's assessment was correct, the interest existed. However, it was unmistakably circumscribed in Erfurt to de jure recognition and nothing else. Whether this narrowly defined interest could ever be extended into areas which were closer to Bonn's concept of "normalization" remained an open question after Erfurt. But the eventual success of Brandt's German policy hinges on this question. These were the meager results of a policy which was launched with so much fanfare and which was supposed to put intra-German relations into motion.

There were even more negative aspects of Erfurt and Kassel. At Erfurt Brandt abandoned former positions without compensation, and thus weakened Bonn's bargaining position. However, the "20 points" which Brandt presented at Kassel as a basis for a contractual adjustment between the two states were a drastic departure in a negative direction from his former policies.[37] It was said that in order to make intra-German relations more dynamic it would be necessary to throw some ballast overboard. It is no exaggeration to say that at Kassel virtually all ballast was jettisoned. The "20 Points" fulfilled all the demands of the Ulbricht regime, short of de jure recognition and even that remained a question of mere formality. After stating in Point Number 5 that each state is independent and autonomous in "affairs affecting their internal sovereign authority," Brandt recognized the exclusive sovereignty of Ulbricht in East Germany. Bonn's long-contested "insufferable tutelage" over East Germany was also abandoned in Point Number 6. Furthermore, in order to formalize the relations of the two states Point Number 19 proposed the exchange of plenipotentiaries of ministerial rank who were to be "accorded with all

Brandt, Chancellor of the Federal Republic of Germany, March 19, 1970, in Erfurt," in *ibid.*, pp. 11–33.
36. "Joint Communiqué, March 19, 1970, in Erfurt," *ibid.*, p. 48.
37. "Statement of the Federal Chancellor Willy Brandt at the Morning Session," *Kassel . . .* , *op. cit.*, pp. 13–15.

the necessary facilities and *privileges*" (italics added). Moreover, although the language of Point 20 remained vague, it offered a regulation of the question of membership of the two states in international organizations, and would undoubtedly have opened the door to the United Nations, a longtime desire of the GDR.

One of the most important concessions made by Brandt was contained in Point 13. The proposed stipulation mutually to examine "spheres of clashes" between the two national legislatures coupled with an "endeavour to remove clashes in order to avoid disadvantages for citizens of both States" amounted to much more than the removal of past "discriminatory legislation." For all practical purposes, in Point 13 Bonn accepted the right of the GDR to interfere in its domestic affairs. One may doubt that the qualification, "in this connection [both states] will start from the principle that on each side the sovereign authority is restricted to its national territory" would be an adequate safeguard. However, concessions can be made not only by spelling out intentions or including stipulations in a treaty. They can also be made by omissions. There is no reference in Brandt's 20 Points either to the principle of self-determination for the Germans or to its contractual preservation. How was this omission compatible with Brandt's insistence on both the maintenance and the practical application of this principle which he had made only seven months earlier in his governmental declaration? Finally, the greatest concession to the GDR was made at Kassel during the afternoon session, when the Chancellor said that ". . . I am convinced that in the course of time the problems you characterize as international recognition of the German Democratic Republic can also be settled."[38] One has only to compare this with Brandt's former statement "for us the recognition of the GDR under international law is out of the question"[39] to see how slippery the road of unilateral concessions can be.

38. "Statement by Chancellor Willy Brandt at the Afternoon Session," *Kassel . . .* , *op. cit.*, p. 52.
39. This statement was contained both in the governmental declaration and in the first State of the Nation message. See: *Regierungserklärung, 1969 . . .* , *op. cit.*, p. D500 and "Verpflichtung zur Wahrung . . . ," *op. cit.*, p. 51.

Negative and unpromising as the results of Erfurt and Kassel may have been they did not affect the ultimate outcome of Bonn's negotiations with Moscow which was a far more important part of Brandt's *Ostpolitik*. It is not necessary to describe here either the negotiations or the accompanying speculations. Suffice it to say that on August 12, after seven months of hard bargaining, which was conducted in carefully guarded secrecy, a treaty was signed between the Soviet Union and the Federal Republic.[40] The Bonn-Moscow Treaty has been hailed as a formidable contribution to East-West reconciliation, as a milestone toward *détente*, and as the beginning of a new epoch in which the *impediments* of antiquated prejudices have been replaced by the sober appreciation and acceptance of political realities. Undoubtedly, the significance of the most important document of the postwar era should not be underestimated. Nor should one minimize the importance of an agreement between Europe's leading military power and Europe's leading economic power. Yet neither the stipulations of the Treaty itself, nor subsequent Soviet behavior seem to have justified the euphoria which had accompanied the Treaty's conclusion.

In his televised address from Moscow, Chancellor Brandt said: ". . . nothing is lost with this treaty that was not gambled away long ago."[41] This statement may be literally true, although neither the SPD nor the FDP can claim innocence in the so-called "gambling away" process. However, politics is a quid pro quo business and a closer look at the Treaty and at the accompanying documents reveals that in the Bonn-Moscow agreement the "quid-s" by far outnumber the "quo-s". Thus, the contracting parties proceed in the Treaty from "the acceptance of the existing situation" in Europe (Art. 1), a statement which clearly implies the contractual recognition of the status quo, a long-time objective of Soviet foreign policy. It further stipulated a mutual renunciation of the use of force

40. For the official documentation of the Treaty, the accompanying speeches, declarations and comments of both the government and opposition, see *The Treaty of August 12, 1970, between the Federal Republic of Germany and the Union of Soviet Socialist Republics* (Press and Information Office of the Federal Government, Bonn, 1970).
41. "Address on television by the Federal Chancellor from Moscow," *The Treaty . . . , op. cit.*, p. 25.

insofar as both states pledge to "settle their disputes exclusively by peaceful means . . . pursuant to Article 2 of the UN Charter (Art. 2)." Furthermore, the Treaty contractually finalizes the European boundaries which have existed since World War II by declaring them inviolable, by pledging to respect them unrestrictedly, and by mutually renouncing any territorial claims in Europe (Art. 3).

There are several questions raised by the Treaty which still remain unanswered. Most important among them is the question whether or not the Soviet Union has in fact fully renounced its alleged right to use force with regard to West Germany. Legally speaking, the answer to this question remains at best inconclusive. The Soviet claim to use force against West Germany has always been based on the so-called "enemy states clause" contained in Articles 53 and 107 of the UN Charter, of which the latter is the more important. Unfortunately, the Bonn-Moscow Treaty makes no reference to either of these Articles. There is only a pledge to settle future disputes between Bonn and Moscow according to Article 2 of the UN Charter. Yet from a purely legalistic point of view Article 2 does not nullify Article 107 which *expressis verbis* says that "Nothing in the present Charter shall invalidate or preclude action . . ." against former enemy states. Thus as long as Article 107 is not amended or expressly nullified, the right of the Soviet Union to take unilateral action against West Germany remains, at least theoretically, still valid. Even if one abstains from such legalistic hair-splitting, there remains a certain amount of ambiguity with regard to this particular clause of the Treaty. Is there any assurance that in the future Moscow will not again denounce the West German government as fascist, militaristic and imperialist, as it did in 1967, in order to uphold its barely renounced claim to intervene? Is there any assurance that the interpretation of the Treaty will be the same in Bonn and in Moscow? Unfortunately, the answers to these questions are negative.

The second question left unanswered by the Treaty is the issue of German reunification. The Treaty does not explicitly prohibit the reunification of Germany, but this possibility is virtually excluded by (1) the contractual acceptance of the "territorial integrity of all states in Europe" and by (2) recognition of the inviolability of "the frontiers of all states in Europe including . . . the frontiers between the Federal Republic of Germany and the German Democratic Republic (Art. 3)." The so-called "German option" contained in a letter delivered to and officially accepted by Gromyko does not change this fact.[42] It is true that by accepting the "Letter on German Unity" the Kremlin acknowledged as valid Bonn's political objective to "work toward a state of peace in Europe in which the German nation will recover its unity in free self-determination." However, there are at least two considerations which render this part of the Bonn-Moscow agreement virtually meaningless. First, a "state of peace in Europe" as envisaged by Moscow does not include a reunited Germany. It is even questionable whether a normalization of relations in the Western sense of the word between the two German states would be tolerated by Moscow. Second, the Kremlin cannot in the foreseeable future shelve its two states theory without alienating the ruling elite in East Germany. The political existence of this elite depends on a permanent division of the nation; its survival is of vital importance for the maintenance of the Soviet Empire in Eastern Europe.

In contrast to the ambiguity surrounding the renunciation of the use of force clause and the sterile "German option," the Treaty has clear-cut advantages for Moscow of considerable magnitude. First, Bonn's unequivocal acceptance of the inviolability of the frontiers of third states confers upon Moscow a kind of protective function with regard to these states, thus demonstratively recognizing the Kremlin's hegemonial position in Eastern Europe. Second, by means of the Treaty the Soviet Union has for the first time obtained an important contractual legitimation of the status quo. Third, due to this fact the Treaty enormously strengthened Moscow's bargaining position in any future European security arrangement to which Western Europe has at least theoretically already subscribed. Finally, by omitting the most important question, the status of West Berlin, the Treaty has left the Soviet Union with a political

---

42. "Letter on German Unity," *The Treaty . . .* , *op. cit.*, p. 10.

leverage of utmost importance in this unsolved problem.

On balance, the Moscow Treaty seems to constitute something less than a success for Bonn. The Moscow agreement does not (either by itself or coupled with any future treaties between Bonn and Eastern Europe) represent the beginning of a process which would lead to the breakthrough in the East for which many West German foreign policy makers have hoped. The Moscow Treaty with all its implications is at best a very modest success for Willy Brandt's government.

It is true that, after several years of agonized soul-searching and failure of political imagination with regard to the East, West German leadership has successfully reformulated its policy. Its former approach, which aimed at the reunification of the country through strength, has been replaced by a policy of reconciliation with the East. Neither the Great Coalition nor the Brandt-Scheel government could, to be sure, accept the division of the country under international law. Reunification and preservation of the nation's unity remained the ultimate, though increasingly elusive, objective of German foreign policy. However, Bonn's Eastern and German policies were to be a clear-cut constructive policy which would attempt to deal realistically with the developments of the last two decades instead of with the immediate consequences of the war.

Thus from 1966 on, in acordance with Germany's historical tradition and under the pressure of internal and external factors, Bonn turned its attention increasingly toward Eastern Europe. The foreign policy has sought to dispel distrust in the East, and change widespread misconceptions concerning German foreign policy objectives. Bonn has furthermore learned that it cannot play Eastern Europe off against the Soviet Union, nor can it make a deal with the Kremlin at the cost of the East European states. What Bonn could and did do was increase its political and economic activity in this area.

The most important limiting factor continues to be the Soviet Union itself. Its predominance in Eastern Europe allows it to exercise a decisive political influence in Eastern Europe. Moreover, during the last two decades the USSR has integrated the East European states into the Soviet economic system. Military integration has also advanced, and these client states have become heavily dependent on Soviet military might. All this implies that important political decisions can be made only at Moscow's indulgence, and major political moves on the part of the East European state must be aligned with the overall foreign policy aims of the Soviet Union. Yet during the 1960's there appeared a multitude of signs which indicated certain structural and ideological changes in the Eastern bloc along with clearly discernible permissiveness on the part of the Soviet Union. Hungary's partly liberalized political and economic system, Rumania's considerable independence in foreign policy and trade decisions, and the overall tendency toward limited economic pluralism, grudgingly tolerated or hesitantly encouraged by most East European leaderships, seemed to indicate a transformation of the Eastern bloc and a decline of Soviet influence in the area. Moreover, the unbearable economic plight of increasingly consumption-oriented societies, a malaise which the Soviet Union was unable to remedy economically and unwilling to do so for political considerations, prompted the East European states to turn toward the West.

As a result of these factors, during the last few years great hopes were entertained in the West for the liberalization process in Eastern Europe. Western observers have hoped that continuous liberalization pressures will weaken the political, ideological and economic bonds between the Soviet Union and her client states. The inference was that the more liberal the East European countries became, the more amenable they would be to Western approaches, including those from Germany. However, the assumption that these changes will be so profound as to result ultimately in a liberal social, economic and political order is a dangerous misconception. Moreover, any assumption that the Soviet Union will tolerate the continuation of a development which by definition might strike at the foundations of the socio-economic structure of the communist societies is unjustified. Nevertheless, the West's "relaxation policy," of which Bonn's policy is an integral part, is still partly based on these assumptions.

Those who believe that the policy of relaxation could result in a kind of *détente-entente-cooperation* in Europe are victims of self-deception. We are told that the Soviet Union no longer is a threat to Western Europe. We are also told that with the acceptance of the status quo (which will eventually be formalized in a European security arrangement) the Soviet Union has become a satisfied power. We are further told that greatly expanded economic relations will further develop the communist economies and will further liberalize their societies, thus lessening the gap between the two halves of divided Europe. Moreover, it is said that permanent economic cooperation will result in economic interdependence which in turn will lessen political tensions. Finally, we are told that only through political accommodation and economic cooperation could we arrive at a lasting settlement in Europe.

All this may be true, but there is reason to doubt it. While the Western European states, including the Federal Republic, may feel secure and are taking advantage of the stalemate between the two superpowers, the build-up of a formidable Soviet naval force continues undiminished. Soviet military power remains geared to maximize the position of the USSR in the world. While Western societies anticipate social changes in the communist world, the Soviet Union still regards even the mere existence of non-communist orders as "ideological aggression." Jointly-built factories, long-term credits and the general modernization of the socialist economies with Western help may satisfy the rising consumer demands of the East Europeans and Russians. But this will also enormously strengthen the system itself domestically. Moreover, the modernization of the East European economies will strengthen their interdependence and cohesion. Furthermore, the acceptance of the status quo does not miraculously eliminate tensions — it may only temporarily defuse them. Nor does present Soviet diplomacy indicate that the alleged Soviet readiness for a European security arrangement represents more than a *tactical* change in the otherwise inflexible strategy of Soviet foreign policy.

A second political factor limiting Bonn's policy is the nature of Moscow's relationship with East Germany. Under the Ulbricht regime the GDR became indispensable to the Soviet Union in many ways. Politically, the very existence of the GDR ensures the continued division of Germany. Militarily, East Germany is an outpost of Moscow's defensive and offensive strategy. Economically, the GDR is Moscow's most important single trading partner; it is Eastern Europe's most important industrial supplier, and the increasing integration of its economy with that of the Soviet Union furnishes an example to be emulated by other COMECON countries.

Undoubtedly the pre-condition for a lasting settlement between Bonn and Moscow (and thus with Eastern Europe) is mutual willingness to compromise. The area where the Soviet Union could and should make compromise in order to make the present attempt at reconciliation meaningful is the German question and the still pending problem of Berlin. However, even if the Kremlin should be willing to compromise, its freedom to make concessions is seriously limited. After the signing of the Moscow Treaty it was suggested that Ulbricht would be put under pressure by Moscow to make his own contribution to *détente* by modifying his intransigence toward Bonn. So far there is no sign that Moscow has applied such pressure, and there is no indication that it will do so in the foreseeable future. The very indispensability of the GDR to Moscow makes it unlikely that the latter will ever pressure Pankow to make concessions which could be detrimental to the GDR's international position or which could endanger the political stability of the regime and the hard-won domestic tranquillity of its society. It is equally unlikely that the Soviet Union will deviate from the established principles of its own German policy, the "two states theory," the demand for full diplomatic recognition of the GDR, and the retention of West Berlin as a separate political entity.

After many years of rethinking and after many substantial concessions to the Soviet Union, the division of the German nation into two states is still a permanent feature of the European scene; it will continue indefinitely. Moreover, Bonn's Eastern policy is very likely to suffer serious setbacks in the future, and may well end in stalemate. Will the ensuing frustrations and disappointments create serious crises for West German democracy? Could the sad experience of the ill-fated Weimar Republic be repeated? Fortunately, such developments are unlikely. There is no alienation in the Federal Republic of Germany today comparable to the malaise that per-

vaded the Weimar Republic. That democracy and parliamen-
tarism in West Germany are currently criticized is in itself a
healthy sign.

The Federal Republic enjoys peace, order, and prosperity,
and Bonn's sincerity in attempting to create a new opening to
the East is not open to serious question. However, at the present there is no common denominator between West Germany
and the Soviet Union, and it is questionable whether the latter's
political attitude will drastically change in the foreseeable
future. To ensure success in future dealings with the Soviet
Union, East Germany and Eastern Europe, Bonn will not only
need to have its conciliatory attitudes reciprocated from the
East, but will also need continuous and strong political and
moral support from the West. In the final analysis it is the
attitude of powers greater than West Germany which will
decide the future of Central and Eastern Europe.

At the same time Bonn's Eastern policy must be carried out
within the context of the West's policy of *détente*, for which the
outlook is grim. The Western powers seem to ignore the fact
that differences between their systems and the communist states
are not a matter of nuance. They are fundamental. Only the
tactics but not the overall strategy of Soviet foreign policy have
changed in the last fifty-three years. Today the Kremlin seeks to
achieve its goals by indirect means, by maneuvering its oppon-
ents into a series of partial political capitulations. One must
hope fervently that present accommodations, advantageous as
they may now seem to Western Europe, will not be condemned
by future generations: for voluntarily accepting the present
situation could easily be the first step toward involuntarily
accepting eventual Soviet political and military hegemony
over the entire European continent.

selected
bibliography

Documents, official publications and speeches

Aktive Aussen- und Innenpolitik (Kiesinger's interview on West German television), Bulletin of the Press and Information Office of the Federal Republic of Germany, No. 29, March 21, 1967

Aktive Ostpolitik der Bundesregierung, Bulletin of the Press and Information Office of the Federal Republic of Germany, No. 26, March 14, 1967

Berlin als Brücke zwischen West und Ost (Kiesinger's interview with the *Berliner Morgenpost*), Bulletin of the Press and Information Office of the Federal Republic of Germany, No. 24, March 5, 1967

Dem Wohle beider Teile unseres Volkes dienen (Kiesinger's speech before the *Bundestag*), Bulletin of the Press and Information Office of the Federal Republic of Germany, No. 63, June 19, 1967

Denkschrift der Evangelischen Kirche in Deutschland über die Lage der Vertriebenen und das Verhältnis des deutschen Volkes zu seinen östlichen Nachbarn, Verlag des Amtsblattes der Evangelischen Kirche in Deutschland, Hanover, 1965

Der deutsch-sowjetische Meinungsaustausch zur Frage des Gewaltverzichts, Europa Archiv, August 25, 1968

Der Politik der Gewaltlosigkeit Überzeugungskraft verleihen (Kiesinger's interview with the *Deutschlandfunk*), Bulletin des Presse- und Informationsamtes der Bundesregierung, No. 12, February 8, 1967

Die Politik des Gewaltverzichts, Presse und Informationsamt der Bundesregierung (Bonn, 1968)

Dokumente zur Ostpolitik der Bundesregierung, Europa Archiv, April 25, 1970

Dortmunder Parteitag der Christlich Demokratischen Union, *Rede des Herrn Aussenministers Dr. Gerhard Schröder*, Parteivorstand der CDU, Bonn, 1962

Einladung zur Teilnahme an der Tausendjahrfeier der Christianisierung Polens in Tschenstochau im Jahre 1966, Katholische Nachrichtenagentur, Dokumentation, Nr. 34, December, 1965

Entschlossenes und konsequentes Handeln der Regierung (Kiesinger's speech before the *Bundestag*), Bulletin of the Press and Information Office of the Federal Republic of Germany, No. 22, March 1, 1967

Erfurt March 19, 1970, A Documentation, Press and Information Office of the Federal Republic of Germany, Bonn, 1970

Erklärung der deutschen Bundesregierung zur Deutschlandpolitik, Bulletin of the Press and Information Office of the Federal Republic of Germany, No. 38, April 14, 1967

Erklärung der Teilnehmerstaaten des Warschauer Vertrags vom 6. Juni, 1966, Europa Archiv, August, 1966

Erklärung der Teilnehmerstaaten des Warschauer Vertrags vom 6. Juli 1966 zur europäischen Sicherheit, Europa Archiv, Vol. 21, pp. D414–24

Erklärung des deutschen Bundeskanzlers vor dem Bundestag am 1. Februar 1967 über die Aufnahme diplomatischer Beziehungen zu Rumänien, Bulletin of the Press and Information Office of the Federal Republic of Germany, No. 11, February 21, 1967

Erklärung für den Frieden und Sicherheit in Europa (Bucharest), Europa Archiv, Vol. 22, pp. D259–66

Friedensaufgaben der Deutschen (Kammer der Evangelischen Kirche in Deutschland für öffentliche Verantwortung), Europa Archiv, Vol. 23, No. 12, June 25, 1968

Für eine dauerhafte und gerechte Friedensordnung (Kiesinger's speech before the *Bundestag*), Bulletin des Presse- und Informationsamtes der Bundesregierung, No. 10, January, 1967

Für menschliche Erleichterungen im geteilten Deutschland (Kiesinger's address on West German television), Bulletin of the Press and Information Office of the Federal Republic of Germany, No. 63, June 19, 1967

Gemeinsame Erklärung der kommunistischen und Arbeiterparteien nach ihrer Konferenz in Pressburg am 3. August 1968, Europa Archiv, Vol. 23, No. 16, August, 1968

Gemeinsamer Brief an die kommunistische Partei der Tschechoslovakei, Neues Deutschland, No. 197, July, 1968

German Polish Dialogue, Atlantic Forum, Bonn, Brussels, New York, 1966

Germany's Position and Germany's Future. Address by Dr. Gerhard Schröder at the 11th Federal Congress of the Evangelical Circle of the CDU/CSU parties, Press and Information Office of the Federal Republic of Germany, Bonn, April 7, 1964

Government Statement made by Chancellor Ludwig Erhard in the Bundestag on October 18, 1963, Press and Information Office of the Federal Republic of Germany, October, 1963

Interview of Willy Brandt with "Welt am Sonntag" on January 8, 1967 as reprinted in Bulletin of the Press and Information office of the Federal Republic of Germany, No. 3, 1967

Kassel, May 21, A Documentation, Press and Information Office of the Federal Republic of Germany, Bonn, 1970

Kommuniqué über die Konferenz der Aussenminister der Mitgliederstaaten des Warschauer Paktes, Europa Archiv, Vol. 22, pp. D123–4

"*Making Europe a Whole: An Unfinished Task*" (*address by Lyndon B. Johnson*), Department of State Bulletin, Vol. LV, No. 1426, October 24, 1966

Manifest der Nationaldemokratischen Partei Deutschlands. Vorstand der Nationaldemokratischen Partei Deutschlands, Hamburg, 1965

Mit Ernst und Redlichkeit der Freiheit und Einheit unseres Volkes dienen (Kiesinger's address to the *Bundestag*), Bulletin of the Press and Information Office of the Federal Republic of Germany, No. 64, June 20, 1967

Neujahrsbotschaft des Staatsvorsitzenden, Walter Ulbricht, Europa Archiv, February, 1966

Neujahrsbotschaft des Staatsvorsitzenden der DBR, Walter Ulbricht, vom December 31, 1966, Europa Archiv, Vol. 22, pp. D102–4

Points of Main Emphasis in German Foreign Policy, Address by ·Dr. Gerhard Schröder at the General Meeting of the Iron & Steel Industry Association in Düsseldorf, June 28, 1963, Press and Information Office of the Federal Republic of Germany, Bonn, 1963

Rede des deutschen Bundesministers des Auswärtigen vor der beratenden Versammlung des Europarats am 24. Januar, 1967, Bulletin des Presse- und Informationsamtes der Bundesregierung, No. 8, Jan. 26, 1967

Rede des sowjetischen Aussenministers, Andrej Gromyko, am 9. Dezember 1965, Europa Archiv, February, 1966

Rede des tschechischen Schriftstellers Ludvik Vaculik, Osteuropa, Vol. 18, No. 3, March, 1968

Rede des Vorsitzenden des Staatsrates und ersten Sekretär der SED am 21. April, 1966 in Berlin, Europa Archiv, June, 1966

Regierungserklärung von Bundeskanzler Willy Brandt vor dem Deutschen Bundestag am 28. Oktober, 1969, Bulletin des Presse- und Informationsamtes der Bundesregierung, No. 132, October 29, 1969

Regierungserklärung von Bundeskanzler Dr. Kurt Georg Kiesinger vor dem Deutschen Bundestag am 13. Dezember, 1966, Bulletin des Presse- und Informationsamtes der Bundesregierung, No. 157, Dezember 14, 1966

Resolution of the Central Committee of the Rumanian Communist Party on the Consultative Conference in Budapest, Agerpress "Documents, Articles, and Information on Rumania", No. 6 Supplement, March, 1969

Soll die Politik Bonns fortgesetzt werden? Pressedienst, Institut für Demoskopie, Allensbach, 1963.

The Action Program of the Czechoslovak Communist Party, Europa Archiv, Vol. 23, No. 13, July, 1968

"*The Outlook for Freedom*" (*address by Dean Rusk*), Department of State Bulletin, Vol. LV, No. 1425, October 17, 1966

The Treaty of August 12, 1970 between the Federal Republic of Germany and the Union of Soviet Socialist Republics, Press and Information Office of the Federal Republic of Germany, Bonn, 1970

Twelfth Annual Conference of NATO Parliamentarians, November 14–19, 1966, Reports, Resolutions, Recommendations, NATO, International Secretariat, Paris, 1966

Weitgespannte Politik des Friedens und der Verständigung (Kiesinger's address to the 84th session of the *Bundestag*) as reprinted in Bulletin of the Press and Information Office of the Federal Republic of Germany No. 6, 1967

Wiedervereinigung: Grösstes Anliegen der jungen Generation, Pressedienst, Institut für Demoskopie, Allensbach, 1965

Wortlaut der Sowjetnote an die Bundesrepublik und des Friedensvertragentwurfes vom 12. März 1959, Europa Archiv, November 10, 1959, D13251–64, 1959

Wortlaut der Sowjetnote an die Vereinigten Staaten, Frankreich, England und die Bundesrepublik am 10. März, 1952, Europa Archiv, 5 D10115–22, 1952

SECONDARY SOURCES

Books

Bender, Peter, *Offensive Entspannung: Möglichkeit für Deutschland*, Kiepenheuer (Cologne–Berlin, 1969)

Brandt, Willy, *A Peace Policy for Europe*, Holt, Rinehart and Winston (New York, 1969

Brandt, Willy, *The Ordeal of Coexistence*, Harvard University Press (Cambridge, Mass., 1964)

Brentano, Heinrich von, *Germany and Europe*, Fred A. Praeger (New York, 1964)

Brzezinski, Zbigniew, *Alternative to Partition*, McGraw Hill Book Company (New York, 1965)

—— *The Soviet Bloc, Unity and Conflict*, Frederick A. Praeger (New York, 1967)

Collier, David S. and Glaser, Kurt (ed.), *The Conditions for Peace in Europe*, Public Affairs Press (Washington, D.C., 1969)

—— *Western Policy and Eastern Europe*, Regnery (New York, 1966)

Dehio, Ludwig, *Germany and World Politics in the Twentieth Century*, W. W. Norton and Company (New York, 1967)

Domes, Alfred (ed.), *Entspannung, Sicherheit und Frieden*, Verlag Wissenschaft und Politik (Köln, 1968)

Dönhoff, Marion, Rudolf Walter Leonhardt and Theo Sommer. *Reise in ein fernes Land — Bericht über Kultur, Wirtschaft und Politik in der DDR*, Nannen (Hamburg, 1964)

Dulles, Eleanor, L., *Berlin: The Wall is not Forever*, University of North Carolina Press, (Chapel Hill, 1967)

Epstein, Klaus, *Germany After Adenauer*, Foreign Policy Association (New York, 1964)

Erler, Fritz, *Ein Volk sucht seine Sicherheit*, Europa Verlagsanstalt (Frankfurt/M, 1961)

For Peace and Equality — For the Universality of the UN, German League for the United Nations (Dresden, 1966)

Grewe, Wilhelm, G., *Deutsche Aussenpolitik der Nachkriegszeit*, Deutsche Verlagsanstalt (Stuttgart, 1960)

Griffith, William E. (ed.), *Communism in Europe*, 2 vols., M.I.T. Press (Cambridge, Mass., 1966)

Grosser, Alfred, *Die Bonner Demokratie*, Karl Rauch Verlag (Düsseldorf, 1960)

Guttenberg, Karl-Theodor Freiherr von und zu, *Wenn der Westen will: Plädoyer für eine mutige Politik*, Seewald Verlag (Stuttgart, 1964)

Hacker, Jens, *Die Rechtslage Berlins — Die Wandlungen in der sowjetischen Rechtsauffassung*, Deutscher Bundesverlag (Bonn, 1965)

Hanrieder, Wolfram F., *West German Foreign Policy, 1949–1963*, Standford University Press (Stanford, California, 1964)

Hartman, Frederick, H., *Germany Between East and West*, Prentice Hall (Englewood Cliffs, N.J., 1965)

Hiscocks, Richard, *The Adenauer Era*, Lippincott (Philadelphia, 1966)

Holbick, Karel and Henry Myers, *Postwar Trade in Divided Germany — The Internal and International Issues*, The Johns Hopkins Press (Baltimore, 1964)

Jaksch, Wenzel, *Westeuropa — Osteuropa: Perspektiven wirtschaftlicher Zusammenarbeit*, Atlantic Forum (Bonn, 1965)

Jaspers, Karl, *Freiheit und Wiedervereinigung*, Piper Verlag (Munich, 1960)

—— *The Future of Germany*, The University of Chicago Press (Chicago, 1967)

—— *The Question of German Guilt*, Capricorn Books (New York, 1961)

Kaiser, Karl, *German Foreign Policy in Transition: Bonn betwzen East and West*, Oxford University Press (New York, 1968)

Kindleberger, Charles, P., *International Economics*, Richard Irwin (Homewood, Ill., 1958)

Kitzinger, U. W., *German Electoral Politics*, The Clarendon Press (Oxford, 1960)

Klafkowski, Alfons, *The Potsdam Agreement*, Panstowe Wydawnitcwo Nankowe (Warsaw, 1963)

Klefisch, Johannes W., *Schluss mit Deutschland*, Verlag Wissenschaft und Politik (Cologne, 1963)

Klemperer, Victor, *Die unbewältigte Sprache*, Metzler Verlag (Darmstadt, 1966)

Knütter, Hans-Helmut, *Ideologien des Rechtsradikalismus im Nachkriegsdeutschland*, Röhrscheid Verlag (Bonn, 1961)

Koch, Thilo, *Wohin des Wegs Deutschland? — Ein Wiedersehen*, Kindler Verlag (Munich, 1965)

Kogon, Eugen, *Die unvollendete Erneuerung: Deutschland im Kräftefeld, 1945–1963*, Europa Verlag (Frankfurt/M, 1964)

Kraus, Herbert, *Der völkerrechtliche Status der deutschen Ostgebiete innerhalb der Reichsgrenzen nach dem Stande vom 13. Dezember 1937*, Schwartz (Göttingen, 1964)

Kuby, Erich, *Das ist das Duetsche Vaterland: 70 Millionen in zwei Wartesälen*, Schertz and Goverts (Stuttgart, 1957)

Legien, R. , *The Four Power Agreements on Berlin — Alternative Solutions to the Status Quo?* Carl Heymanns Verlag (Berlin, 1961)

Littel, Robert, *The Czech Black Book*, Frederick A. Praeger (New York, 1969)

London, Kurt, *The Permanent Crisis*, 2nd edition, Blaisdell Publishing Company (Waltham, Mass., 1968)

Majonica, Ernst, *Deutsche Aussenpolitik — Probleme und Entscheidungen*, Kohlhammer Verlag (Stuttgart, 1965)

Maras, Joachim and Päschke, Hans (ed.), *Deutscher Geist zwischen Gestern und Morgen*, Deutsche Verlagsanstalt (Stuttgart, 1954)

McInnis, Edgar, Hiscocs, Richard and Spencer, Robert, *The Shaping of Postwar Germany*, Frederick A. Praeger (New York, 1960)

Meissner, Boris, *Russland, die Weltmächte und Deutschland — Die sowjetische Deutschlandpolitik, 1943–1953*, Nolke (Hamburg, 1953)

Merkl, Peter, *Germany: Yesterday and Tomorrow*, Oxford University Press (New York, 1965)

Neal, Fred Warner, *War and Peace and Germany*, Norton (New York, 1962)

—— *Offensiver Auseinandersetzung*, Pressestelle des Vorstandes der SPD, Vorwärts Druck (Bonn, 1966)

Planck, Charles R., *Changing Status of German Reunification in Western Diplomacy*, The Johns Hopkins University Press (Baltimore, 1967)

Plischke, Elmer, *Governments and Politics of Contemporary Berlin*, Nijhoff (The Hague, 1963)

Richardson, James L., *Germany and the Atlantic Alliance — The Interaction of Strategy and Politics*, Harvard University Press (Cambridge, Mass., 1966)

Richter, Ernst, *Das zweite Deutschland — Ein Staat der nicht sein darf*, Mohn Verlag (Gütersloh, 1964)

Schlamm, William S., *Germany and the East–West Crisis*, McKay (New York, 1959)

Schmidt, Helmut, *Defense or Retaliation — A German Contribution to the Consideration of NATO's Strategic Problems*, Oliver and Boyd (Edinburgh and London, 1962)

Schröder, Gerhard, *Decision for Europe*, Lawrence Verry (Mystic, Conn., 1964)

Schütz, Wilhelm Wolfgang, *Das Gesetz des Handelns — Zerrissene Einheit unserer Welt*, Scheffler Verlag (Frankfurt/M, 1958)

—— *Die Stunde Deutschlands — Wie kann Deutschland wiedervereinigt werden?* Deutsche Verlagsanstalt, (Stuttgart, 1954)

—— *Reform der Deutschlandpolitik*, Kuratorium Unteilbares Deutschland (Berlin, 1965)

—— *Rethinking German Policy*, Frederick A. Praeger (New York, 1967)

—— *Schritte zur Wiedervereinigung*, Mutterschmidt Verlag (Göttingen, 1959)

—— *West-Ost Politik*, Vandenhöck und Ruprecht (Göttingen, 1963)

Selucky, Radoslav, *Reformmodel CSSR, Entwurf einer Sozialistischen Marktwirtschaft*, Rowohlt Verlag (Hamburg, 1969)

Sethe, Paul, *Zwischen Bonn und Moskau*, Scheffler Verlag (Frankfurt/M, 1956)

Shulman, Marshal D., *Stalin's Foreign Policy Reappraised*, Harvard University Press, (Cambridge, Mass., 1963)

Smith, Jean Edward, *The Defense of Berlin*, The Johns Hopkins Press (Baltimore, 1963)

Speier, Hans, *Divided Berlin* — *The Anatomy of Soviet Political Blackmail*, Frederick A. Praeger (New York, 1961)

—— *Germany, the Continuing Challenge*, Rand Corporation (Santa Monica, Calif., 1966)

Stahl, Walter, *The Politics of Postwar Germany*, Frederick A. Praeger (New York, 1963)

Stehle, Hansjacob, *Nachbar Polen*, Fischer Verlag (Frankfurt/M, 1963)

—— *The Independent Satellite : Society and Politics in Poland since 1945*, Frederich A. Praeger (New York, 1965)

Strauss, Franz Joseph, *The Grand Design*, Frederick A. Praeger (New York, 1965)

Studnitz, Hans-Georg von, *Bismarck in Bonn* — *Bemerkungen zur Aussenpolitik*, Seewald Verlag (Stuttgart, 1964)

Száz, Zoltán M., *Germany's Eastern Frontiers*, Regnery (Chicago, 1960)

—— *The German People and the United Nations*, German United Nations League, Verlag Zeit im Bild (Dresden, 1966)

Váli, Ferenc A., *The Quest for A United Germany*, The Johns Hopkins Press (Baltimore, 1967)

Windsor, Philip and Roberts, Adams, *Czechoslovakia 1968, Reform, Repression and Resistance*, Columbia University Press (New York, 1969)

Wiskemann, Elizabeth, *Germany's Eastern Neighbours*, Oxford University Press (London, 1956)

Wolfe, James, *Indivisible Germany: Illusion or Reality?* Martinus Nijhoff (The Hague, 1963)

Wolfers, Arnold, *Germany, Protectorate or Ally?* Yale University Press (New Haven, Conn., 1950)

Zeman, Z. A. B., *Prague Spring*, Hill and Wang (New York, 1969)

Articles

Acheson, Dean, "Europe: Decision or Drift?" *Foreign Affairs* (January, 1966)

—— "Withdrawal from Europe? 'An Illusion'," *New York Times Magazine* (December 15, 1963)

Allardt, Helmut, "Deutschland und Polen," *Aussenpolitik* (May, 1963)

Bechtold, Heinrich, "Kiesinger und die deutsche Aussenpolitik," *Aussenpolitik* Vol. 17, No. 12 (December, 1966)

—— "Ulbrichts Niederlage in Osteuropa," *Aussenpolitik*, Vol. 18, No. 3 (March, 1967)

Billington, James H., "Force and Counter-Force in Eastern Europe," *Foreign Affairs*, Vol. 47, No. 1 (October, 1968)

Bregman, Alexander, "Germany's Search for an Eastern Policy," *East Europe* (March, 1966)

Bryant, Christopher, "Prague Summer," *East Europe*, Vol. 17, No. 9 (September, 1968)

Brzezinski, Zbigniew, "The Danger of a German Veto," *The New Leader* (January 20, 1964)
—— "The Framework of East-West Reconciliation," *Foreign Affairs*, Vol. 46, No. 2 (January, 1968)
—— and Griffith, William E., "Peaceful Engagement in Eastern Europe," *Foreign Affairs* (July, 1961)
Cameron, James, "A Shadow no longer than a crooked Cross," *The New York Times Magazine* (September 11, 1966)
Churchill, Winston S., "Mein Grossvater ist für sie ein Kriegsverbrecher," *Der Spiegel* (January 9, 1967)
Dönhoff, Marion, Gräfin von, "Ein Anfang ist gemacht," *Die Zeit* (February 17, 1967)
—— "Ein Konzept für Deutschland," *Die Zeit* (March 1968)
—— "Vorbild Preussen?" *Die Zeit* (February 21, 1967)
Gamarnikow, Michael, "Eastern Partners of Western Businessmen," *East Europe*, Vol. XIV (September, 1965)
Görgey, László, "Emerging Patterns in West German-East European Relations," *Orbis*, Vol. X, No. 3 (Fall, 1966)
—— "New Consensus in Germany's East European Policy," *The Western Political Quarterly*, Vol. XXI, No. 4 (December, 1968)
Gross, Hermann, "Wirtschaftssysteme und Wirstschaftspolitik der Südosteuropäischen Staaten," *Südost Europa Jahrbuch* (München, 1966)
Hadik, Laszlo, "The Process of Détente in Europe," *Orbis* (Winter, 1970)
Hamm, Harry, "The Rumanians Bravely Pursue an Independent Line," *Frankfurter Allgemeine Zeitung* (March 4, 1968)
Hermann, Kai, "SED 7th Congress Caught Napping," *The German Tribune*, No. 264 (April 29, 1967)
Holesovsky, Vaclav, "Prague's Economic Model," *East Europe*, Vol. 16, No. 2 (February, 1967)
Höfer, Werner, "Sie wollen den Bonnern Beine machen," *Die Zeit* (November 15, 1966)
Kahn, Herman and Pfaff, William, "Our Alternatives in Europe," *Foreign Affairs*, Vol. 44, No. 4 (July, 1966)
Kanturek, Jiri, "Reform: Full Victory or Hesitant Steps?" *Kulturni Tvorba* (January 5, 1967)
Knight, L. E., "Czechoslovakia's Fading old Guard," *East Europe*, Vol. 16, No. 11 (November, 1967)
Kolkowitz, Roman, "Spezifischer Funktionswechsel des Warschauer Paktes," *Aussenpolitik*, Vol. 20, No. 1 (January, 1969)
Komocsin, Zoltán, "Patriotism, National Interest, Internationalism," *Problems of Freedom and Socialism* (June 10, 1966)
Kovalov, S., "Suverenitat i internationalnye obzajannosti socialisticeski stran," *Pravda* (September 26, 1968)
Krucky, Joseph, "Upsurge in Czechoslovakia," *East Europe*, Vol. 17, No. 9 (September, 1968)
Kühnl, R., "Neofascism on the Rise," *Review of International Affairs*, Belgrade (February 20, 1967)

Kuznetsov, Vladle, "With a Long-Range Aim," *The Current Digest of the Soviet Press*, Vol. 20, No. 38

Lauen, Harald, "Osteuropa unter dem Zugriff der Hegemonialmacht," *Europa Archiv*, Vol. 23, No. 20 (October, 1968)

Lemberg, Hans, "Die Intervention in Prag: Stationen, Ursachen — Ein erstes Fazit," *Osteuropa*, Vol. 18, No. 10/11 (October, November, 1968)

Lias, Godfrey, "Satellite States in the Post-Stalin Era," *International Affairs*, London (January, 1954)

Lippmann, Walter, "Too Good to be True?" *Newsweek* (January 30, 1967)

London, Kurt, "Entspannung und Friedensstrategie: Entspannung als Methode oder Endziel?" in Domes, Alfred (ed.), *Entspannung, Sicherheit und Frieden*, Verlag Wissenschaft und Politik (Köln, 1968)

Mahnke, Heinrich, "Die Deutschland-Frage in den Freundschafts- und Beistandspakten der DDR mit Polen und der CSSR," *Europa Archiv*, Vol. 22, No. 9 (May 9, 1967)

Mätzke, E. O., "Die Antwort der Ungefragten," *Frankfurter Allgemeine Zeitung* (March 22, 1966)

Mehnert, Klaus, "Der Moskauer Vertrag," *Osteuropa* (December 12, 1970)

Meissner, Boris, "Soviet Concepts of Peace and Security," in Collier, D. S. and Glaser, Kurt (eds.), *The Conditions for Peace in Europe*, Public Affairs Press (Washington, D.C., 1969)

Münchmeyer, Alwin, "Ausweitung des Osthandels — Aber wie?" *Aussenpolitik* (July, 1965)

Neumann, E. P., "Steckbrief einer radikalen Partei," *Die Zeit* (January 24, 1967)

Pollock, James, "The West German Electoral Law," *The American Political Science Review*, Vol. 48, No. 2

Pospielovsky, George, "Geistige und politische Auswirkungen der Sowjetischen Wirtschaftsreform," *Osteuropa*, Vol. 18, No. 2 (February, 1968)

Razumovski, Andreas, "Die Wachablösung," *Osteuropa*, Vol. 18, No. 3 (March, 1968)

—— "Rechtsradikalismus in der Bundesrepublik im Jahre 1966," *Politik und Zeitgeschichte* (June 14, 1967)

Schütz, Wilhelm Wolfgang, "Was ist Deutschland? Denkmodelle für eine deutsche Gemeinschaft," *Kuratorium Unteilbares Deutschland* (Berlin, 1968)

Schweisfurt, Theodor, "Moskauer Doktrine und sozialistischer Internationalismus," *Aussenpolitik*, Vol. 19, No. 12 (December, 1968)

Shawi, Nikola, "Internationalism and the Cause of Peace," *The Current Digest of the Soviet Press* (November, 1968)

Shub, Anatole, "Prague: Euphoria of Revolution," *The Washington Post* (March 15, 1968)

Shulman, Marshall D., " 'Europe' versus 'Détente'," *Foreign Affairs*, Vol. 45, No. 3 (April, 1967)

Smith, Canfield F., "The Rocky Road to Unity," *East Europe*, Vol. 18, No. 2 (February, 1969)

Smith, Jean Edward, "Our View of a Stagnated East Germany is Dated," *The Washington Post* (April 16, 1967)

Sommer, Theo, "Bonn Changes Course," *Foreign Affairs*, Vol. 45, No. 3 (April, 1967)
—— "Denken an Deutschland," *Die Zeit* (March 14, 1966)
—— "Ein Dialog zwischen Deutschen," *Die Zeit* (March 25, 1966)
—— "Kein Alibi für Nichtstun," *Die Zeit* (January 14, 1967)
—— "Politik ohne Gänsefüsschen," *Die Zeit* (February 12, 1968)
—— "Rückblick auf ein 'deutsches Jahr'," *Die Zeit* (February 2, 1971)
Stehle, Hansjacob, "Botschafter nach Budapest?" *Die Zeit* (January 31, 1967)
Studnitz, H. G. von, "Deutschland zwischen den Mächten," *Aussenpolitik* (August, 1956)
Süsking, Walter E., "Der politische Rohstoff," in Moras, Joachim and Paschke, Hans, *Deutscher Geist zwischen Gestern und Morgen*, Deutsche Verlagsanstalt (Stuttgart, 1954)
Svitak, Ivan, "Before the Occupation: The Political Crisis in Czechoslovakia," *East Europe*, Vol. 17, No. 10 (October, 1968)
Szulc, Tad, "A Spring of Freedom is Cut Short in Czechoslovakia," *The New York Times* (September 1, 1968)
Triska, Jan, "The Party Apparatchik at Bay," *East Europe*, Vol. 16, No. 12 (December, 1967)
Un groupe de recherches, "Model de sécurité européenne," *Centre d'études de Politique Étrangère*, Vol. 32, No. 2
Urban, Rudolf, "Der verwegene Geist: der 10. Kongress tschechoslovakischer Schriftsteller und seine Folgen," *Osteuropa*, Vol. 18, No. 3 (March, 1968)
Viney, Deryck E., "Der Demokratisierungsprozess in der Tschechoslovakei," *Europa Archiv*, Vol. 23, No. 12 (June, 1968)
Wagner, Wolfgang, "Überprüfung des deutschen politischen Instrumentariums: Die Hallstein Doctrine nach Ulbrichts Besuch in Aegypten," *Europa Archiv* (March, 1965)
—— "Voraussetzungen und Folgen der deutschen Ostpolitik," *Europa Archiv* (September 10, 1970)
Zehrer, Hans, "Die polnischen Bischöfe," *Die Welt* (December 4, 1965)
Zoll, Werner, "Über den Wert der Hallstein Doktrin," *Aussenpolitik* (September, 1966)
Zundel, Rudolf, "Gemischte Gefühle in Bonn," *Die Zeit* (January 14, 1967)

Unsigned Articles

"Anmerkungen zum Manifest und zu den Grundsätzen der NPD," *Deutsche Nachrichten* (January, 1967)
"Bemühungen Pankows um eine kommunistische Aktionsfront," *Neue Zürcher Zeitung* (January 2, 1967)
"Bonns innerdeutsche Entspannungspolitik," *Neue Zürcher Zeitung* (April 18, 1967)
"Deutscher Nationalismus — Marke NPD," *Neue Zürcher Zeitung* (November 25, 1966)

"Deutschlandpolitik im Zeichen der Entspannung," *Neue Zürcher Zeitung* (April 2, 1967)

"Der Dienst ist mir absolut zu schlapp," *Der Spiegel* (February 13, 1967)

"Ein Paar hunderttausend Bauern wählen NPD," *Der Spiegel* (February 13, 1967)

"Europa endet nicht mehr an der Elbe," *Die Zeit* (July 9, 1965)

"Im Bundestag wird alles anders aussehen" (Spiegelgespräch mit dem NPD-Vorsitzenden Adolf von Thadden), *Der Spiegel* (May 26, 1969)

"Keine Beseitigung der Differenzen in Warschau," *Neue Zürcher Zeitung* (February 1, 1967)

"Noch ist Poland nicht gewonnen," *Die Welt* (November 25, 1964)

"Novotny Speaks," *East Europe* (December, 1965)

"Ostblock verstärkt Angriffe auf Bonn," *Die Welt* (October 15, 1965)

"Rapacki in Paris," *Neue Zürcher Zeitung* (January 27, 1967)

"Rapackis Pariser Gespräche," *Neue Zürcher Zeitung* (January, 30 1967)

"Sondernummer: Ungarn," *Industriekurier* (March 8, 1965)

"Sondierungen Lahrs in Budapest," *Neue Zürcher Zeitung* (January 24, 1967)

"Umgekehrte Hallstein Doctrine," *Neue Zürcher Zeitung* (January 8, 1967)

"Vertriebene protestieren gegen EKD-Denkschrift," *Die Welt* (October 17, 1965)

German, Hungarian and Polish Newspapers and Periodicals

Aussenpolitik (West Germany)
Christ und Welt
Der Monat
Der Spiegel
Deutsche Aussenpolitik (East Germany)
Die Welt
Die Zeit
Europa Archiv
Frankfurter Allgemeine Zeitung
Frankfurter Rundschau
Kulturni Tvorba
Literarny Novini
Magyar Hirek
Magyar Nemzet
Népszabadság
Neue Zürcher Zeitung
Neues Deutschland (East Germany)
Osteuropa
Pravda
Süddeutsche Zeitung
The German Tribune
Tribuna Ludu
Ziczie Warszawi
Zolnierz Volnosci

index